William T. Tilden

HOW TO PLAY
BETTER TENNIS

Cornerstone Library   *New York*

Reprinted 1975

This new Cornerstone Library edition is published by arrangement with Simon and Schuster, Inc., and is a complete and unabridged reprint of the hardcover edition.

To Art
   whose willingness to study and work inspires me to write this book with the sincere hope and belief that he will be world's champion.

Bill

CORNERSTONE LIBRARY PUBLICATIONS
Are Distributed By
Simon & Schuster Inc.
630 Fifth Avenue
New York, New York 10020

Manufactured in the United States of America
under the supervision of
Rolls Offset Printing Co., Inc., N. Y.

TABLE OF CONTENTS

ABOUT THE AUTHOR

Early in 1950, the Associated Press conducted a poll of 391 sports writers, to determine the greatest tennis player of the past 50 years. Bill Tilden received 310 ballots, with his closest rivals, Jack Kramer and Donald Budge, polling 32 and 31 votes respectively.

Anyone who ever saw Tilden play tennis is almost certain to agree with the results of this landslide vote. His record has never been equaled in all tennis history. From 1920, when he first won the National Singles Championship, through 1930, when he retired from Amateur tennis, he was ranked officially as the Number One player in the United States each year. In eight of those years he was also universally recognized as the World's Champion, and in all eleven of them he served as a member of this country's Davis Cup teams.

Seven times the National Singles Champion, he also won the British Singles Championship on each of the three occasions when he made the trip to compete at Wimbledon. His individual Davis Cup record shows seventeen victories as opposed to only five defeats.

He was co-holder of the National Doubles Championship four times, and helped win five Davis Cup doubles matches while only losing two. He took the National Clay Court Championship six times running, and at one time or another (and usually several times), he held every title worthy of mention on all surfaces and in every country where tennis is played as a major sport. In addition, since turning Professional, he has won all the important titles in those ranks, including both singles and doubles championships of the United States, England, and several other countries.

FOREWORD

This book is intended for tennis players. If you are not a tennis player in the sense that you love the game—its technique, its tactics, its psychology, and its ethics—do not attempt to read it. If, however, you are one of the real tennis nuts—and they are legion—this is written for you in the hope that it may fill a real want. In it I am attempting to give all I have learned of the game over the past half century. If from its pages one player learns something of value that will lift him from just a person who hits a tennis ball to that very different status—a tennis player—I am indeed rewarded.

WILLIAM T. TILDEN, 1950

PART ONE

THE FOUNDATIONS OF TENNIS

CHAPTER 1

A Viewpoint on the Game

IT WAS just a half century ago that I lifted a tennis racquet for the first time and, with dire results, hit my first tennis ball. There was something about the delightful sound of ball on gut, even if slightly marred by the jingle of glass from the broken window, that entered my soul with a never-to-be-forgotten thrill. It was a new emotion to my six years, but one that now, at fifty-six, still carries the thrill—even if not the broken glass. I can, at least, hit the ball in the court most of the time.

I urge you—play tennis! Tennis is the most valuable sport that any individual can learn, even more so than golf. It is the most universally played of all athletics, and its rules are the same the world over. A good game of tennis is the open-sesame on every continent and in almost every nation. Language is no barrier to tennis players, since whether a ball is out or in can be seen and understood without spoken words. Individual sport is always more valuable than team sport in adult life, since team sport requires too much effort to organize in the press of the business world. Tennis, by its small requirements of time and playing space, and its comparatively inexpensive equipment, lies within the reach of practically everyone. The tremendous increase in public courts in almost all cities has taken the game away from the classes and put it in the hands of the masses, which is a healthy and splendid thing in every way. Even our schools and colleges, steeped in the English tradition of team sport rather than individual sport, are gradually yielding to pressure and giving more and more importance to tennis. The steady growth of tennis courts at schools and colleges, together with the increase in the number that provide professional coaching for their students, shows that at last the importance of the individual sport for the adult life of the citizen of the future has been recognized by our educators.

Certainly the greatest benefit that tennis gives its follower is the means to keep physically fit. It is a game that can be played practically from the cradle to the grave—and it is apt to aid in postponing the latter many years. I started to play tennis at the age of six—and I was not unique in that. King Gustav of Sweden was still playing in his late eighties. I remember a few years ago watching a doubles match at The West Side Tennis Club at Forest Hills, between four men who met about three times a week to fight it out—and the combined age of the quartet was three hundred years. It is a game that can be carried on along with practically any form of human endeavor. The businessman, doctor, lawyer, actor, singer, writer, etc., are all able to find enough leisure time to play and, by so doing, increase their productivity by better physical condition.

The better one plays tennis, the greater its rewards, materially, spiritually, and psychologically. The champion, whether he is the champion of the world or just champion of the particular city block where he lives, is a big man in his own world and carries added weight socially and in every other way. The great players who attain international fame gain rewards in travel and the chance to meet peoples of other lands that no amount of money could buy. I would not trade the great people I've met, or the wonderful places I've visited through my tennis, for all the money in the world.

Therefore, I urge all who can to play tennis, and if you do play it, play it to the very best of your ability and opportunity. Enjoy it as a game, keep it a sport. If you become great in it, the material rewards will come to you without your playing it with that in mind. Sometimes I feel that the game has become too commercialized today. It may still be called Amateur, but it has been organized into Big Business, which, in turn, has taken away much of the sporting element and made it too grim and serious.

Most people who take up tennis seem to feel that it isn't worth the effort unless they can master the game in a short time. I can only say that I have never discovered any short cut to learning tennis. I feel that the player who is willing to learn slowly and soundly from the basic foundation of the game will benefit in the end. He will go ahead far faster than one who superficially picks up a flashy but unsound style in a short time, and then stops working. Weeks spent in laying a sound groundwork of correct strokes at the start will save years in the end.

There is nothing mysterious about tennis. It is a game of sound, scientific principles that anyone with an average mind and body can learn to play well if he will take the trouble to work at it. The great champions are not born but are made by their own—and at times their coaches'—efforts. In the years I have played tennis, I have looked for a born tennis player, but I have yet to find one. The best I have been able to do is to find a gifted athlete, but only long, hard work made the player. The two greatest naturals in tennis I ever saw were Vincent Richards and Frank Kovacs, yet neither had quite the willingness to do the long serious practice work that produces a champion of champions, and an all-time great.

I believe one can learn to play tennis in a year or less—but it takes five years to make a Tennis Player and ten years to make a Champion. Much that is the trouble with tennis today is due to the unwillingness of promising youngsters to go through the proper preparations in laying a sound, scientific foundation. The result is that once the first flush of youth and athletic prowess starts to fade, the modern game disintegrates because it has no solid and intelligent foundation on which to depend. Speed and power are essential in the equipment of every great player, but they alone cannot suffice. Attack alone, or defense alone, is not enough; a combination of the two, with the knowledge of how to employ them, is what makes your F. J. Perry Ellsworth Vines, Jr., Donald Budge, or Bobby Riggs. It was not until Jack Kramer added defense to his attack in his professional tour with Riggs that he established himself as the outstanding player of the world.

The success of the California game of hard hitting as exemplified by

Vines, Budge, and Kramer might have done serious damage to the total picture of tennis if it had not been offset by the equal success of the subtleties and intellectual defense of Perry and Riggs. But all these great stars produced their outstanding performances only after learning the incontrovertible lesson that the combination of attack and defense, in proper blend, is the maximum in tennis skill. The reader may feel that this explanation should come as a summing up to this book, but to me, if the proper picture is drawn at the beginning, then all that follows takes its place in logical order within the frame. The player who really desires to go high must have an ethical and technical background that will explain the game of today. The champion of today owes his game to the champions of yesterday, just as he will add his bit to the champion of tomorrow. The wise student should learn all he can about the styles and methods of the great players of the past, every bit as much as he does of the players of the present.

It is the fashion of the moment to view with patronizing contempt, as slightly obsolete, the game of any player who has been in the tennis world for a decade. As for anything older than that, the modern youngster either knows nothing or considers it a dead issue. Where would our culture, education, and art be if this became the fashion in these worlds? Why, then, should we ignore our valued heritage in athletics? School and college coaches should hold regular classes in their sports that would provide accurate knowledge on the changing methods of their game, and of the great stars of the past. I often hear youngsters come out with remarkable but half-baked discoveries of shots or their uses that have been perfected and played years before by great stars of the past. Think how much trouble those boys or girls would have been saved if a coach had told them so, and gone on to explain correct technique.

There is nothing that Jack Kramer does today that players of the past have not done equally well. There are some very valuable things of the past that have been lost in the wild scramble for speed and power. These should be recovered and brought back into the repertoire of the modern player.

Much of the present-day type of tennis is due to the effect of the official propaganda of the United States Lawn Tennis Association on young players. During the past two decades the U.S.L.T.A. has built up the finest and best-organized junior development system of any nation in the world. Much of our international success has been due to this, since we have encouraged and increased competition among our boys and girls from their earliest teens. By so doing, we have ingrained the spirit of competition, developed the will to win, and given the opportunity for champions to mature. Naturally, along with all its virtues, such a large organizational plan would also develop its attendant weaknesses, chief of which is the armchair theorist, who crept into power and established himself as a coach or tennis expert. Often he is merely an interested, well-meaning crackpot, who knows little or nothing about the actual development of the tennis game from either its technical or its tactical side. These earnest but incompetent people take immediate result rather than sound development as their criterion of correct method, often without ability to see below the surface, to the foundation. The success of such hard hitters as Vines, Budge, and Kramer so impressed these armchair coaches that they induced the U.S.L.T.A. to start a steady stream of propaganda to its juniors that, summed up in a few words, amounts to "Hit like hell and run to the net." The result of this method, used almost exclusively by these inexperienced and unwise coaches, is that from 1940 to 1950 junior tennis has steadily declined in class in the United States, although more of it is played than ever before. The year 1949 set a new low in the standard. It is amazing how far this blindness will carry these armchair coaches. I know of one high-ranking official, who has never been better than a third-class club player, but whose word is taken as gospel by the juniors in his district, who seriously advises his young players, "Never think on a tennis court—just hit as hard as you can and run to the net." How can real tennis players develop under that sort of official advice? The immediate result, which anyone who knows anything about tennis technique can see at first glance, is the deterioration of all ground strokes among the youngsters of today. This is particularly true of that basic shot, most important stroke in tennis, the forehand drive. There are many well-produced

9

backhands, but even these are inclined to be unsound and too aggressive. The defensive chop and the medium pace and slow drive have practically disappeared from the game, and all one sees is a bunch of kids trying to reach the net behind shots that are pitifully uncertain. If almost all these kids were not amazing volleyers and servers, they would have no chance at all, and, in fact, they have none now when they meet a really first-class ground-stroke player like Perry or Riggs, who can also volley when needed.

The official attitude of the U.S.L.T.A. should be overhauled and modified. The need of attack should definitely be stressed to all young players, but not overstressed as it is today. If the line of learning, and the method of teaching it, could be set by a group of such great stars as Eleanor Tennant, Vincent Richards, Fred Perry, Alice Marble, Donald Budge, and Bobby Riggs, rather than by such unpractical theorists as do it today, the standard of junior tennis would start an immediate rise and in a comparatively short time reach a new peak. The group of advisers I mentioned are all professionals, and today co-operation between the amateur body and the professionals is almost completely lacking, but there is no reason why it should be. It is my belief that all these pro stars and many others, myself included, would gladly give their knowledge and experience to aid the youngsters of the United States to improve their games. If, for any reason, the U.S.L.T.A. did not wish to accept their help gratis, the Association is financially able to pay for it. It is a situation where pride or prejudice should not be allowed to stand in the way of co-operation. Something drastic is needed to bring back a balanced and intelligent method to American tennis, and to take full advantage of the wealth of superlative material that is today only realizing a small fraction of its true worth. I see boys and girls with wonderful natural ability held back and practically condemned to mediocrity because they are almost forced along a path that can only develop a portion of their abilities. It is a crying pity that this is so, when it could be avoided by a wise advisory method. The predominance of the California group, where tennis is played on concrete courts, is partially responsible for the overstress on attack. On concrete, cement, and asphalt, power pays off while defense and finesse are almost useless. Yet less than 5 per cent of all world tennis is played on such hard courts. Over 85 per cent is played on some form of clay or dirt court, while grass, with its 10 per cent, is still the most important surface, since the United States, English, and Australian Championships are all played on it. On grass, and even more definitely on clay courts, defense and finesse, variation of spin, speed, pace, and depth have equal importance with sheer power. All of those players whose goal is international competition should recognize that they must not allow themselves to be held within the limitation of the game as played generally in their home locale. Just as California and the Pacific Coast overstress attack, so do the East, South, and Middle West place too much reliance on defense. The wise player attempts to learn both styles, since in major competition only a blend of both can carry a man to the very top.

It is a pity that so far nothing has really been done to standardize court surfaces. The greatest single step forward that tennis could take would be for the International Tennis Federation to adopt one standard surface as the only one on which recognized tournaments could be held. It will never be. England, Australia, and to a lesser degree the United States would fight to hold grass as the standard, yet grass is impossible to grow in many countries where tennis is very popular. Some form of clay, like En-Tout-Cas, or dirt, is a possibility and even practical almost all over the world, but the tendency of this surface to slow up the game—overstress defense and underplay attack—makes it far from universally popular. Even within a great country like the United States, various sections have such definite prejudices that they would battle to protect their own favorite type of court. I am positive it would take more than a major earthquake ever to wean California away from the hard court. It is sincerely believed—and possibly correctly, though I doubt it—that much of that state's success is due to the hard court. Personally, I think it is the fact that the climate allows all-year play, coupled with splendid organization of tennis, that keeps California at the top in this country. After all, Oregon and Washington have the hard courts, as do Arizona and New Mexico, but they haven't the other two factors.

Therefore, just so long as a tennis player will be called upon to play on varied court surfaces, just so long must he strive to have a real all-court game capable of meeting all conditions with the best possible style of play.

Everything today points to one thing. Too much emphasis is laid on physical effort, quick result, and snap judgment. In the increased rush of modern living, the need for thoughtful, careful planning and preparation has been overlooked and sacrificed. Too great publicity on victory, and not enough appreciation for the sound, complete artist, has built up a fear of immediate defeat in many of our young players. So they are not willing to work slowly toward a real goal. Everything I write here about tennis today is written in the hope that the young-sters who read this book will gain the knowledge that there is no need for all the rush toward immediate success.

Tennis should always be played with the head consciously direct-ing the racquet. Every shot should be played with a definite intention behind it, one that will make it of value to the player who hits it.

The viewpoint on tennis that stamps a tennis player is that the game is a science and an art. It can reach its highest expression only if a player is willing to study and practice in an attempt to master the game in all its varied facets. In the coming pages I will try to show as much of the game as I have been able to learn in fifty years. I need at least that much more time to learn all there is to know. What I have learned I owe to those who preceded me, my own contemporaries, and those who have followed me. Do not scorn to learn from those you can beat. There is much to be learned from them. Remember al-ways that even more can be learned in defeat than in victory, if you suffered that defeat when you gave your best. And keep in mind that, no matter how great you are, there is always the possibility of some-one greater.

CHAPTER 2

Concentration; Practice;
The Racquet Head and the
Preparation of the Shot

Concentration. Learning is a habit that can be acquired. There are certain great aids to learning that any good coach or teacher knows, and tries to instill in a pupil at the very beginning. Chief among them is concentration. A person who really learns to concentrate, so that the mind does not wander to extraneous things during study, can do a job in about half the time that the person of average attention can. In tennis, concentration is vital to learning the game—and, once learned, even more vital in playing it. The man who keeps his mind fixed on his match at all times puts a tremendous pressure on his opponent. Anyone who ever played against Frank Parker, or, in the old days, René Lacoste, knows what a tremendous strain is placed on him by the unwavering pressure of concentration from across the net. I have always believed that it was his lapses of concentration at points in every big match that kept Frank Kovacs from reaching the absolute peak.

Most people only actually and accurately hear about half of what is told them, and guess at the rest. Unfortunately, in learning the fundamentals of the game, half is not enough. The first thing every young player should learn to do is listen intently to *all* that is told him. Once he has really heard it, then comes the big job—he must translate the words into action. His mind must govern his muscles to follow the directions. The greater the concentration of the mind on the job, the quicker is the groove of physical control established.

What so often happens is a quick superficial learning, followed by the inevitable reaction that comes from thinking the thing is learned before the actual groove is set. Every coach sees it and should help his pupil guard against it. The first day or two in teaching a new stroke sees a remarkable improvement in the pupil. The novelty of it holds his interest and keeps his power of concentration high, so that progress is easy to see. The third day usually brings the relapse. The novelty has worn off, the physical groove has not yet solidified quite enough to hold, and the interest is probably slightly waning as the pupil wants to get ahead to something else. Result: concentration slackens, mind wanders, and the physical responses are unco-ordinated and undisciplined. That is the moment when the wise coach and the clever pupil pull the whole picture together by added concentration, and start to form the sound habit of learning. Concentration, and only concentration, will lift the pupil from the rut. There are many pitfalls that lie in wait to trip the player who allows his concentration to wander while he is learning the fundamentals. He may grow careless about keeping his eye on the ball, changing his feet, controlling his weight, getting his racquet head back, or deciding on his shot and its direction. Failure of any one of these will cause him to make errors. The concentration that has become instilled so deeply that it becomes almost instinctive allows a player to make specific decisions in plenty of time. The first great fundamental of tennis is to train yourself to concentrate so that you never stop concentrating while on the court. This applies when you are learning the technique of the game, when practicing shots or playing in practice, but above all, when playing matches.

Practice. Young players dislike to practice shots today more than anything in the game. Once they have the general technique in hand, they are willing to let their instinctive sense of hitting a ball develop their shots rather than go through the grind of practice—of hitting the same stroke over and over again until mechanically it is almost instinctive. That is why one sees so few players today with real control, yet such practice is necessary to achieve a complete command of technique. Frank Parker, as a boy, spent hours daily just practicing shots, which is why he has held his position near the top of the tennis world so many years. René Lacoste, the morning of the day he met Jean Borotra in the finals of the United States Championship in 1926, spent one solid hour standing on the court tossing lobs until he could drop a ball within a foot of the baseline. That afternoon Borotra rushed the net, only to chase those lobs back to the baseline time and again. So deadly was Lacoste's control of the lob that he ran through Borotra in three straight sets. It is the willingness to practice, as Lacoste and Parker did, that is lost today, and must be regained if we are to develop players of absolutely top rank. Only by complete concentration on the job at hand can such work be done and done right.

The Racquet Head. Before I turn to the actual fundamentals of stroke production, I want to go into what is of almost equal importance, since it applies to all strokes in tennis, namely, the all-important fact that it is the head of the racquet and only the head of the racquet that returns a ball in tennis. Only by proper and early preparation for a shot is it possible to use that racquet head correctly.

Power—speed and pace—is controlled completely by the manner in which the head of the racquet is swung against the ball in hitting it. Body movement and weight are secondary to, though interrelated with, the racquet swing. The player who will always have his racquet head hit the ball solidly and travel directly *into* and *through* the line of his shot will always have complete control of his strokes. If he is able to do this at all times, he is even able to hit off the wrong foot with good results, as Fred Perry does on his famous forehand. The reason that correct footwork is so vital to good stroke production is that correct footwork furnishes an automatic way to bring the racquet head into a position to hit directly into and through the line of the stroke. Once the feet are so placed that the body is in correct position, the less deliberate body movement or foot movement there is, the better—*provided* the player hits freely with the head of his racquet and

15

does not cramp his swing or shorten its arc by compensating with a wrist wiggle. Service, drive, chop, and smash need only the free arm swing that sends the head of the racquet directly into and through the ball on the line of the intended shot. The volley alone should not carry the long follow-through of the racquet head. The greatest tennis motto I know is "Let your racquet head do your work." There is no need to tie yourself up in knots to hit a ball hard, or to control it. Just swing your racquet head through the ball at the place you want it to go. It will go there, quickly or slowly, according to the speed of your racquet head.

The natural question is: How do I always get my racquet head ready to use in this way? That is where the early preparation of shots comes into its own. Have you ever noticed that you never see a great player look as if he is hurried, no matter how short a time he has to reach a ball, or how far away it is? Yet all the second-string, mediocre players are always scrambling around, scurrying like scared rabbits and working themselves to death. That is because the great player prepares his shot *on the way to it* while the lesser player starts to prepare it *when he reaches the ball.*

Preparation for a Shot. The secret of preparation for a shot lies in taking the racquet head back *the moment* you see where the shot is coming, and holding it in readiness until the time comes to hit the ball. Watch such players as Perry, Riggs, Budge, Kramer, and Parker, and see how they take the racquet back as they move to the ball. The effect is as if the racquet head pulled them into position, instead of their taking position and then moving the racquet. Henri Cochet, the great French star, is a perfect example of this. He almost seemed to aim his shot into your court by using his racquet head to decide on his direction. When I take up the individual strokes, I will speak more fully of the method of early preparation, but as a generality of stroke production, I cannot emphasize too strongly the value of it. It is the secret of all those amazing "gets" that thrill a gallery when a player, running at full speed, reaches a shot that seemed far out of his reach, and passes the net player or hits a clean winner. He made the shot because he took his racquet back *on the way to the ball,* so that when he arrived all he had to do was swing it forward to make the stroke. If his complete preparation had not been made prior to arrival, he would have been unable to swing into the ball and would have been too late to hit it effectively. There are many ways to prepare shots according to the type stroke you decide to play, but the same principle, getting the racquet head back and ready *on the way to the ball,* holds true for all. Only the volley, in which the racquet head is carried *forward* in front of the body so it can meet the ball quickly, is an exception to the rule, but even the volley calls for the same careful preparation on the way, and the same relationship between the racquet head and the ball is present. After all, the gut is put into the racquet to hit the ball with, and that alone will return the ball. So get your racquet head in position to use the gut effectively, and it will help you keep all the unnecessary movements out of your shots.

CHAPTER 3

Condition, Physical and Mental; Equipment

TENNIS matches are won or lost by the sum total of physical condition, courage, intelligence, experience, and stroke equipment of a player. If your sum total is greater than that of your opponent, you win; if it's less, you lose. Luck plays practically no part in the results of tennis matches. There is no game, except chess, where class, or skill if you prefer, tells so consistently. Later I will discuss the value of strokes, and the use of each individually, as well as all those intangible but definitely determining factors of the mind, heart, and body that go to make a champion. But first, there are a few tangible assets that have to be cultivated by any aspirant to tennis excellence, and the outstanding one is to be in good shape.

A healthy mind can exist only in a healthy body. The secret of good physical condition for tennis is moderation. Too much or too little of the natural way of living, excesses or privations, will only result in a condition that most people describe as staleness. Personally, I have always believed that staleness is much more mental and nervous than physical. If you live so carelessly that you get too much food, too much drink, too many excesses of any kind, too little sleep, and couple it with too much physical strain, you will get a violent physical, mental, and nervous upset. I think that few will dispute this. That type of life will make a person not only unfit for athletics but unfit for anything. However, few people stop to realize the dangers of excess in the simple, normal things of life. Too many work along the old Hollywood theory that if one elephant is good, one thousand elephants are a thousand times better. One thousand elephants are likely to be too many, and too much food, sleep, reading, even too much of tennis itself, can do more harm than good.

It is just as dangerous to go to extremes of training. Too rigid training defeats its own purpose by making you too conscious of the sacrifices entailed, upsetting the natural balance of interest that every person should have in life, and allowing the game to get on top of you and rule you. You should keep tennis as a sport, no matter how serious you are in your determination to master it and get to the top. I do not approve of the old "training table rules" for a tennis player. If he were preparing for a short, intensive season of, say, six weeks, it might work, but a tennis player today plays twelve months of the year. It is impossible to stay trained to the second all the time. There must be a period of relaxation and letdown. The clever player learns when and how to do this, without weakening his condition when it should be at its best.

Here are certain generalities about training that can be set down as axiomatic, even though every person is a law to himself when it comes to just when and how to relax:

No athlete should drink alcoholic beverages at all during competition or for a reasonable period before it starts. He is better off not to touch it at any time, for even moderate amounts of alcohol will keep the vision and reflexes uncertain and slow. I think that a player is wise not to use tobacco, but if he does, he should definitely cut it out one month before the peak of his season. Most people are of the opinion that tobacco affects the wind, which to some extent is true, but what is much more serious to a tennis player is that it slows up the speed of the eye.

Plenty of sleep, at least eight to ten hours' average, if possible, should be the goal of an athlete during competition, but that sleep should not be taken at varied and strange hours. The logical way to keep in good condition is to be as regular as possible in your routine without being a slave to it. The young player does well to figure on getting to bed anywhere from ten to eleven o'clock, and being up by eight. It will not produce the same refreshing result if every third night he makes it two to twelve. Do not force yourself to go to bed and try to sleep because the clock strikes ten, if this will make you lie awake and fret over tomorrow's hard match, but at least get in bed and read, or listen to the radio until you feel sleepy. Above all, do not carry today's defeat or tomorrow's battle with you when you go to bed. Today is over. Tomorrow will come soon enough. Brooding over the game at bedtime will get you nothing but worn nerves and slow muscles tomorrow.

Food is another very definite problem for the competitive player. I disagree violently with the old training table idea of rigid diet, little to eat before playing, etc. That is deadly over a long period and often results only in rebellion against the whole game. Eat with intelligence —that is the only restriction I would put on a player. Do not stuff yourself with rich, highly seasoned foods or sloppy indigestible desserts before play. Eat as much as you want at breakfast, lunch, and dinner, but *do not eat between meals* and *do not* fill yourself up with *pop* and *soft drinks* either before, during, or immediately after play. If you must drink soft drinks after play, do it only after you are completely showered and cooled off. The meal before play, usually luncheon, is the most important from the standpoint of your game. Do not fall for the idea that you should not eat a full meal before playing. That's all bunk. You should have plenty of fuel in you. You will burn up a lot of energy in your match. It is better to be slow for a few games at the start because you are full than it is to be weak-kneed and shaky at the climax because you are hungry! The only thing I advise is, try to allow at least an hour from the end of the meal until you play. I've seen so many juniors fill themselves full of hot dogs and pop and go right out and play, and then wonder why they felt badly and got licked. They deserve to lose if they take no better care of their physical condition than that. In my opinion, almost any form of simple plain-cooked food is sensible training. Meat without a lot of "hot" sauces, vegetables, salads, bread, and plain desserts like ice cream, jelly, custards are O.K., but at a meal just before a match I'd cut out dessert. Water is the best drink, with milk a good second. Coffee, tea, and chocolate are all right, if not drunk in too great quantities. I am not in favor of soft drinks with sparkling water because they tend to cause gas and cut your breath. The more regular your eating hours can be, the better for your condition, but you should always be willing to change your eating hour to conform best to your time of play.

I have said that in my opinion staleness is more mental than physical, and I am sure I'm right. I hear people refer to being "overtennised" when I know that they are not averaging more than two sets a day, but they are worrying over their defeats, worrying about whom they may meet tomorrow, who may beat them, worrying over what the press said last week or may say next week. Worrying, worrying, worrying over their game in some form. That person is not "overtennised" in the sense he thinks he is—that he is playing too much; actually he is "undertennised" physically. He is not "match-tough," but he is mentally badly "overtennised." He needs a complete change of interest for a short time, and then a completely new approach when he returns to the game. He has forgotten that tennis is a sport and has lost the ability to have fun playing it. Every player should have some secondary interest to his tennis if he is "majoring" in tennis. He would do well to play cards, or have a hobby like photography, or a love for books or music that can carry him completely out of his tennis world. He might do well to go out and play golf, perhaps very badly, during the period he wants to lay down his racquet. Unless you are a very severe case of "tennis worrier," a layoff of about three days to a week will cure you of the jitters and send you back, racquet in hand, raring to go and playing better than you've played for months. Do not throw your condition to the winds by going on a big bust to break training; you don't need to. A late night or two, a mild party, a lot of laughs, will do it. Once more, moderation and intelligence will solve your problem.

I have always believed that the greatest training and conditioner for any sport is that sport itself. I know that tennis, tennis, and more tennis is the only way I ever reached perfect condition, and I have seen many other players use the same formula. The young players today not only dislike practicing shots, as I have already pointed out. They seem to think they are conditioning if they go out and play a couple of lackadaisical practice sets two or three times a week. I think this accounts for the amazing number who crack wide open in the third set of many of their matches. I cannot see why young men in their middle twenties should show any sign of wear and tear in a five-set match at top speed. I never saw such stars as Henri Cochet, Donald Budge, Frank Kovacs, Fred J. Perry, Bobby Riggs, Gottfried von Cramm, Frank Parker, and Jack Kramer seem in dire danger of physical collapse when they were playing championship tennis in their mid-twenties. Kramer and Kovacs, of course, still are young, but it has only been in the last few years that the others have slipped, even a little bit. Yet Cochet is forty-seven, Perry and von Cramm forty, and Parker, Budge, and Riggs in their thirties. The reason for this is that, as youngsters, all these great stars became match-tough and never lost that quality. The only way to become match-tough is by hard play in practice until it becomes second nature to play and play at top speed. I know what it's worth. In 1927 during the European tour that Frank Hunter and I made, we played five sets of singles in the morning and five sets in the afternoon, every clear day when we didn't have a team match. That practice made Hunter the number 2 singles player in the world and conditioned me so I still owe it a debt of gratitude. One thing that I insist on with my protégé, Arthur Anderson, with whom I have been working for the past five years, is that he play or practice several hours at least six days a week. For two weeks before any important tournament, he plays five sets of singles every day, up to two days before the event starts, and then lays off except for light practice. He is the only junior I know in California who can go at top speed for five sets of singles.

There are very few exercises that really help a tennis player get in shape and stay there. One form of exercise that I strongly urge on a player, particularly if he is inclined to be sluggish or slow in starting, is to skip rope. It is wonderful for the wind and the legs. If it is to do you any good at all, it must be done systematically, and not just now and again. Start slowly for your first week or so. Jump a normal "two-foot" skip, not over ten times without resting, but repeat five separate tens and, if possible, do it morning and evening. Take the ten up to twenty after two days, then in a week to fifty. Once you can do that, begin to vary the type skipping. Skip ten times on one foot, then ten times on the other. Add a fifty at just double your normal speed. Once that is all mastered, then simply take ten minutes in the evening and skip hard, any way you want and at any speed. Let your own intelligence direct you to what gives you the best results. Remember always that stamina is one of the deciding factors in all long, closely contested tennis matches, so work to attain the peak of physical conditioning when you need it most.

Closely allied to physical condition are the equipment you use and the clothes you wear. I am a great believer in comfort in clothes. I like to see the traditional white on the court, with color sometimes used judiciously, but no matter what style clothes, they must be comfortable if you are to play your best. Do not wear too tight things, no matter how much you may want to look trim. Trimness can be achieved with clothes that give you enough room to move without feeling any binding. While I think long trousers on men and skirts on women make the best court appearance, I am of the opinion that sports shorts are the most sensible attire for both. Wear light, cool clothing, using a sweater that can be discarded once you are warmed up. The most important single item is the feet. Be sure to use large enough shoes to give you plenty of room. Cramped toes are not conducive to comfort or speed. Wear heavy wool socks, even in hot weather, since they will take up much of the shock of your running. On hard courts, concrete, cement, asphalt, and wood, I use two pairs of socks and have found that they save my feet very much. Be sure you have a thick rubber sole to your shoe that will protect your foot. Do not use shoes after they start to wear thin or crack. It is foolish economy, for bad feet will beat any tennis player.

I am not going into the matter of the individual make of racquets or balls, beyond the sincere statement that the best racquets, and the balls of all the leading manufacturers, are equally good, and your personal preference for the feel of the racquet should decide which one you use. Mine is a Dunlop Maxply, although I have no connection at this time with the Dunlop Company. Tennis is one game where the little extra spent to get the best pays off with added results, and I urge that all players use the best they can afford.

CHAPTER 4

Keep Your Eye on the Ball

WE ARE NOW ready to take up the specific fundamentals of the game, and the first definite one in tennis is the foundation of all games played with a moving object:

KEEP YOUR EYE ON THE BALL!

I am certain that in every hour I work with a beginner in the game, I repeat this instruction at least thirty times in some form. When I say, "Keep your eye on the ball," I mean watch that ball from the time you first start to toss it to serve until the end of the point, and *never look at anything else.*

Naturally, the pupil decides this is exaggeration, that I am overdoing it. Let me assure you I am not. The pupil always wants to know how he can tell where to hit a ball if he doesn't look over to see. He doesn't need to watch the court. He took a look at it when he went out on it. It is stationary. It isn't going to move off or change its dimensions. The lines are permanent. He knows that the net is in the middle and stands three feet high in the center and three feet, six inches, at the posts, and will not change height during play. The lines, backstops, and sidestops are also fixed in position. They, too, will remain there. Usually you can convince the pupil he need not watch the court or net quite easily, but his next hurdle is far more difficult.

"How about that guy I am playing?" he blurts out. "How can I tell where he is if I don't watch him?"

A reasonable query, certainly, but the answers to it are easy and should satisfy anyone.

First of all you must remember that you are not trying to hit your opponent but to miss him. You are attempting to put the ball where he isn't—not where he is.

"Ah, but I have to see him to know where he is!" cries the pupil. Not at all. If he is a good tennis player, you know where he is without having to see him, because a good tennis player will be in correct position. Correct position for a back-court player is about on the back-line of the court and near the middle of it. If you are facing a net player, his correct position would be about eight feet back on his side of the net, and at a point that would be about two feet toward the center of the court from a straight line drawn parallel to the sidelines from where you hit the ball down through his court. So, if he is a good tennis player you know where he is without having to see him, and if he isn't a good tennis player it doesn't make much difference where he is! After all, the thing you are attempting to hit is a moving ball, which requires the eye to change focus as that ball moves. Obviously, if the eye once loses sight of the ball, it is almost impossible to sight it again clearly in time to hit it cleanly.

The eye functions very much like a camera. Any of us who have ever attempted to take action pictures with a small box camera know of the peculiar results we have produced. One of two things occurs. Usually we get a clear-cut, beautiful picture of the background, with a blurred streak where the moving object—train, car, ball, or what have you—has passed unfocused by the camera eye. Occasionally, we get the reverse, a blurred, muddled background with an apparently stationary, clear object stopped in motion. The eye works the same way when you watch a moving ball coming toward you. You can either see a clear background with a blurred uncertain ball, or a blurred background with a clear ball. In the first instance, your eye has not been kept on the ball during its entire flight, with the result that by the time the ball reaches you, your focus is lost and you will probably mis-hit it. In the latter, the eye is really on the ball and the chances are you will hit it cleanly. When I say, "*Keep your eye on the ball*," I mean actually to include, "*Watch it hit the strings of your racquet*."

Most players watch a ball until it bounces, and then look away as they start to swing, with the mistaken idea that by looking at their opponent's court they will be better able to direct their stroke. Time and again if you watch, you will see a player's head come up to look across the net as he starts to swing, and the resulting shot is mis-hit and usually an error. The average player thinks he can judge the bounce of a ball when it comes off the ground, but he forgets how many things can affect the bounce, any one of which will throw his calculations out of line and make him miss:

1. The ball may have been hit harder or slower than he judged, with the result that it will reach him too soon or too late.

2. It may have been hit with more spin or more subtle twist than he judged, so that the bound goes off line a little more than he expected.

3. The wind may blow the ball off line.

4. The court surface may be rough and the ball may take a bad bound, with the result that once more his guess is bad.

But, if he still has his eye on the ball, he can—perhaps with difficulty, but he still can—get the gut in his racquet head against the ball, and gut, not wood, will return the most shots.

In these days of the modern, net-rushing, power game, the importance of keeping the eye on the ball is growing even greater. One major advantage the net player has against the baseline player is the psychological pressure he puts on the baseliner to look up and see where the net player is. Actually, this is absolutely fatal and results in nothing but a deluge of errors on missed passing shots. When a player sets out to play a passing shot against a net player, he should never see the net player at all. He should make up his mind on which side he will attempt the passing shot, and play it with his eye never leaving the ball. If the net player outguesses him and is in front of it, that is too bad, but at least it puts the burden of making the volley on him, rather than making him the gift of an error from the passing shot. There are certain definite times at which most players are likely to be led into looking away from the ball. The most common occasions involving this error are:

1. Service. Few players actually see their racquet hit their service.

2. Attempting a passing shot. They look up to see the opening.

3. Volleying. They again look up just before they hit the ball, to see in which direction their opponent is moving.

4. Smashing. They look down just before they hit the ball, to see their opponent's court.

Any of these is apt to be at the critical moment of a point. Every player should be most careful to keep his eye on the ball as the climax of each point is reached. When one stops to realize that in first-class tournament tennis about 70 per cent of all points end in error, and that of all errors committed at least 65 to 70 per cent are due to the player's not keeping his eye on the ball, you can readily see why coaches stress to all players, from beginners to champions:

"KEEP YOUR EYE ON THE BALL!"

CHAPTER 5

Footwork and Weight Control

ALL SHOTS in tennis should be hit with the body sideways to the net, and the weight going forward with the shot. The position of the feet is the means by which this is accomplished, and there are definite rules of procedure that will save a pupil months of discouragement. Do not be misled by the fact that many players make fine shots off the wrong foot. They are either naturally gifted "timers," who get the same weight control instinctively, or have so mastered weight control that they can keep their weight in the shot even if caught on the wrong foot. Unfortunately, natural timers are few and far between, so some method must be taught to aid the less fortunate average individual to approach correct timing. The most successful preparation for correct stroke production lies in simplified foot movements, which control body position and weight with the least actual movement.

1. To get to a ball that is any distance away from you, take the first step with the foot that is away from the ball directly across toward the sideline on the side the ball is coming. In explanation, if the ball is coming to your right, step with the *left* foot directly across toward the *right* sideline, pivoting to the right on the sole of your right foot. This will at once turn the left side of the body sideways to the net, and turn your rear end directly away from the ball. If the ball is on the left, step with the right foot across toward the left sideline, pivoting to the left on the sole of your left foot. *Do not step forward in the direction of the net,* since this

will not turn your rear end away from the ball or the body really sideways to the net. It cramps the arm against the body, particularly on the backhand.

BALL COMING TO ONE SIDE OF YOU

Taking it Forehand   *Taking it Backhand*

2. If the ball is coming directly at you, the shot may be played on either side with equal ease. If you desire to hit it on the *right* or forehand, step directly across backward in the direction of the left sideline with the right foot (which is closest to the ball) and pivot to the right on the sole of your left foot. This will turn your rear end away from the ball and the body sideways. If you wish to hit the ball on the backhand, then step across backward in the direction of the right sideline with the left foot and pivot to the left on the sole of your right foot. Do not step in the direction of the baseline behind you, since such a step will not turn your rear end away from the ball, nor will it turn the body sideways.

BALL COMING DIRECTLY AT YOU

Taking it Forehand   *Taking it Backhand*

Remember always to use as few steps and as little movement as possible in reaching correct position. Many times one step, if correctly made with the proper foot, is all that is required. Keep your racquet well extended to reach the ball, in preference to taking too many steps, which will carry you too close to the ball. One of the most common errors of beginners, and, in fact, many tournament players, is to overrun the ball and get so close to it that they cramp their swing and destroy their shot. One universal feature is to be found in the games of all great players. They never seem to be hurried. Watching such stars as Donald Budge, Fred Perry, Bobby Riggs, and Jack Kramer, one gains the impression that they glide or float to the ball. They never rush at it and snap at it. Lesser stars and mediocre players always seem to be going at top speed, but they are often late for the shot. Their racquet work is crowded and hurried. The reason lies in the method of starting footwork. The champion starts with the correct foot and spaces his run so he arrives with the correct foot in position to hit, whereas the average player just runs at the ball to get there any way, without care in preparation on the way over. All footwork should be used to bring the player to the ball with his weight under such good control that he can use it as he wishes when he hits the ball. Whenever it is possible to reach a shot without running, walk to it and keep the body perfectly poised. When the shot requires you to run, do your fast running *first*, so that you can slow up and gain control of your weight and body position before you hit the ball. Never jump or leave the ground with both feet or one foot if you can keep both placed firmly on the ground. The more solidly you are set, the easier it is to hit the ball solidly. The only exception to this is an overhead smash, which, by the very nature of the stroke, high in the air, has a tendency to make the player lift at least one foot. The only effect of leaving the ground with the feet on drives is to dissipate most of the power of the shot, because in the jump the weight goes off the line of stroke, and is not transmitted through the racquet head to the ball.

On any shot where you have to travel sideways to reach the ball, it is natural to step into the ball and keep the body sideways when hitting. It is on the shots when you must move forward or backward that really intricate footwork is needed. When you are forced to run

30

to a short shot on your forehand, or right, come in on the left to about three feet from it, and lean forward with the weight on your left foot. Keep the knees bent, the body quiet as you hit the ball, and *do not bring your body up* with your swing. Let your racquet head do all your work. For the short backhand shot on your left, come in to about three feet to the right of the ball, with knees bent, the weight on the right foot, the right shoulder pointed low directly at the ball, and then hit the ball without body movement and, above all, without letting the body come up with the swing. Let your racquet head do your work. On all short shots guard against the tremendous impulse to look up. Keep your head down and your eye on the ball as you hit it. Only with the feet properly placed, the knees bent, and eye on the ball is it possible to hit low shots effectively.

The deep shot that forces a player to go back with the ball is very difficult and is almost always played incorrectly. Most players run directly across court at the oncoming ball and then turn back with it.

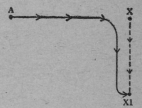

Player at A sees ball about to bounce at X, runs at the place, and then turns back and, while running away from the net, attempts to return ball at X1. By this method, he only manages to tie himself up so he is forced to hit with his weight going away from his stroke.

The correct method is simple, but seldom thought of until too late. It is this:

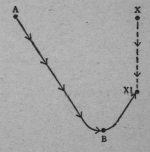

The player at A runs diagonally back to point B behind the oncoming ball, turns and moves in to point X1, where he returns the ball. It is easy to see that he travels about the same distance as in the first case, but here he is moving into his shot, so his weight travels forward with it, and he is not cramped in his swing. The whole theory behind these simple rules of footwork is to allow a player always to be able to *move in* on a ball, so his weight goes *with* his stroke.

We are now ready to go on to the study of the actual strokes, since we have the basic approach to good tennis in mind.

1. Concentrate.

2. Practice.

3. Use the racquet head to hit the ball, and don't try to compensate with the body or the wrist.

4. Prepare the shot early by moving the body into position and getting the racquet head back at the earliest moment.

5. Keep the eye on the ball at all times, actually watching the ball hit the racquet strings.

6. Keep the body sideways to the net in making all strokes, by following the rules given for footwork.

7. Move the weight forward into the shot with the swing.

PART TWO

THE STROKES AND THEIR USES

CHAPTER 6

The General Technique
of All Strokes; The Grips

STROKES are the weapons with which you fight your tennis battles. The better your weapons, the greater the chance of victory. Still, you must always remember that weapons alone never won a war. It is the way in which they are used that determines their usefulness. It is extremely important, almost necessary, to have good strokes, but strokes are not the end—only the means to the end. Therefore, do all in your power to learn good strokes, but never be satisfied to be just a shot maker. Shots alone never won a tennis match or crowned a champion. Above all, never allow yourself to become too stroke-conscious. Correct form is beautiful and a fine thing to attain, but in every important match there is some crucial period where form must go by the board and the result—getting the ball back any way, with two hands and the wood of the racquet if necessary—becomes the deciding factor. So, once more I say work for good strokes in all departments, but always regard them as merely your means to put the ball into the right place at the right time. A badly produced shot to the right place is always better than the most beautiful shot in the world to the wrong place. The first wins, the second loses, so keep your perspective on what strokes mean in tennis.

There are several generalities about strokes that carry through the entire list and should always be borne in mind:

1. For the same effort—the less spin, the more speed, and conversely, the more spin, the less speed. From this it can be seen that the flat shot is almost always the attacking shot, while the spin is more often defensive.

2. On all drives—the racquet head in its backswing should be dropped below the line of the stroke and the ball is struck on the lower outside surface, with the racquet head hitting up on the ball, which gives a tendency toward topspin.

3. On all chops, slices, and volleys, the racquet head should be above the line of the shot in its backswing and hit down slightly on the ball, which gives a tendency toward backspin.

4. On all shots—drives, chops, slices, volleys, smashes, services— the racquet head should hit directly through the ball and at the place in your opponent's court where you wish to place the ball. The secret lies in that geometric axiom, "A straight line is the shortest distance between two points."

Under no circumstances use flourishes or exaggerated movements in stroke production. The essence of good form is absence of "form." Watching all the great stars, you are seldom conscious of what they do before they hit the ball. It is the actual hitting of the ball itself that is important, and that is what sticks in your mind with these players. Everything they do is so simple and natural that it is unobtrusive. Once more you find an example of the simplicity of true greatness. In every form of human endeavor the real masters of the job make whatever they do look so easy. They have eliminated all the waste motion and useless effort, and all that remains is the sheer necessity of their art. That is what really good form does in tennis. Strive to make all your strokes sound, sane, solid, and simply produced. Freak shots, even such remarkable strokes as Pancho Segura's two-handed forehand, or the remarkable two-handed shots of John Bromwich, or the ambidextrous cleverness of Beverly Baker, are never as sound as the orthodox style and will ultimately break up under enough pressure. Stay away from tricks and freak strokes. They won't pay dividends.

In learning strokes the order of work is clear-cut and definite:

1. Learn the correct racquet grips.

2. Learn the correct footwork and body position.

3. Learn to hit the ball.

4. Learn to hit the ball correctly.

5. Learn to hit the ball correctly to a certain place.

6. Learn to hit the ball correctly to a certain place hard, or slow, or at even pace.

THE GRIPS

The first step in acquiring good strokes is to learn the correct grips—notice I said grips, not grip, for no one grip will do for all strokes. You will hear much talk about the three schools of gripping the racquet:

The Eastern grips—which are correct; the Continental grip—which is included in the Eastern style for certain strokes; the Western grip —which is obsolete and discarded today by experts.

Since I am convinced that the Eastern grips are best, I will discuss them only—for in doing so, I bring in the Continental, or Universal, grip where it belongs.

The Eastern Grips. There are three distinct grips within the Eastern school.

1. The forehand drive grip—the key grip from which you learn the others.

2. The backhand drive grip.

3. The Continental grip, or Eastern service, which is used for all strokes *except the drive*.

35

Front view   *Back view*

1. **The Forehand Drive Grip.** Hold the racquet in the left hand so the
short strings are perpendicular to the ground, with the handle point-
ing at you. Then (assuming you are right-handed), place the palm
of the right hand flat against the flat side of the handle at the back
(or right-hand side), away from the direction you would hit the
ball (to the left), so that the handle and your arm make a straight
line. Close the fingers firmly around the handle with the fingers
spread comfortably. Notice that now the face of your racquet and
palm of your hand are in the same hitting plane, and there is practically no broken line at the wrist. This is the key grip of the Eastern
school and is the one that should always be learned first.

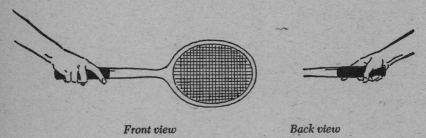

Front view   *Back view*

2. **The Backhand Drive Grip.** Still holding the racquet as described
above, learn the move to the second grip, the backhand grip. Move
the hand backward (or counterclockwise) a quarter-circle turn
until the palm of the hand is *on top* of the handle with the flat side
of the top resting in it, and the arm still making nearly a straight
line with the handle. Close the fingers firmly around the handle
with the thumb *diagonally across* the handle, *not straight up the
back*. In hitting the ball, you use the opposite face of the strings

from the forehand. These two grips, as described, are used to hit all flat and topspin drives, fore- and backhand. They are not used for any strokes except drives.

3. The Continental Grip. This grip, which is also known as the Eastern Service grip or the Universal grip, is used for the chop and slice stroke, the volley, the smash, the lob, and the drop shot, as well as for the slice, twist and cannonball service. It should never be used to drive, particularly off the forehand, where it lacks power. Halfway between the handle positions of the fore- and backhand grips is a slanting surface of the handle. Starting from the original forehand key position, move the hand an eighth-circle turn backward, or counterclockwise (which is half of the way to the backhand grip), until the palm of the hand lies on

Forehand, front view

Backhand, front view

this slanting surface of the handle. Then close the fingers firmly around the handle, let the thumb take a natural diagonal position across the handle, and depress the wrist, making an angle with the handle of the racquet that will bring the head of the racquet above the wrist. The hand in position is not materially changed, only eased between forehand and backhand.

Do not grip the racquet so tightly that it will cramp the arm muscles, but do not go too far the other way by holding the racquet so loosely that it will turn easily in the hand. The time to hold the racquet firmly is at the moment of impact with the ball. Many players feel that they haven't time to change the position of the hand on the racquet handle. Actually, they have more than enough provided they know how to do it. Do not attempt to turn the racquet in the hand but move the hand on the handle, keeping the racquet still. Do this by steadying the racquet in your left hand and moving the right hand into the correct position by sliding it around the handle. Remember that correct grips are a vital part of a sound shot. Even if at first these grips seem slightly unnatural, stay with them until they are mastered. Many players have great difficulty in learning to serve with this grip, because it does not feel natural to them, but let me strongly urge you to stay with it until you have it, since time has proved it is by far the best service grip.

For the sake of continuity, I am writing of service first, for it is the opening stroke in every point in tennis, but in actually coaching the game I advocate learning the forehand drive first, then service, because it is easier to get the feel of the racquet on the forehand. However, in order of learning from a book, the service takes first place.

CHAPTER 7

The Service

THERE are three main types of service in general use, and from them come all the other variations that are of any value. These are:

A. The Slice. This is the most used of any type because it is suited to all sizes of players, and is equally easy for men and women.

B. The Flat or Cannonball. This requires a tall man to control with any speed, and is not of much value to short men or to women.

C. The American Twist, or "Kick." Here is a service that any size man or woman can use, but the amount of physical effort involved for the result gained makes it not a sensible service for most women.

Before I go into the actual stroke production of the three services, I must impress on the pupil several generalities about all types of service. Power and control in service come from the free use of the racquet head, and can never be gained by the wild gyrations and acrobatic writhings in which you see so many players indulge. All of the great services that I have ever seen have been hit with ease, simplicity, apparently little body movement, and no violent contortion. I consider the services of Ellsworth Vines, Lester Stoefen, Donald Budge, Gottfried von Cramm, and Jack Kramer outstanding examples of service, yet the impression of ease of delivery is found with them all. Notice the ease of Bobby Riggs' service in marked contrast to the labored style of Frank Parker. Anyone who has played them both can tell you how much more difficult Riggs' delivery is than Parker's. The secret of the power and control of all these stars lies in the way in which they control their body weight on firmly planted feet, and their unhampered use of the racquet with a free arm swing that carries smoothly through its entire arc, directly at their opponent's court.

To serve well, you must learn to throw well. That is one reason why so few women have really good services. A woman's arm is so set at the shoulder that it will not throw freely. Actually, a service is nothing more than throwing the flat strings of the racquet head against the ball at a point in the air as high as you can comfortably reach. Watch any good baseball player throw a ball and you will see little body movement, no violent contortions, but lots of free arm motion. Just so should a tennis player, serving, impress the watcher. If I find a pupil having trouble learning a service swing, I hand over an old "beat-up" racquet frame and make the pupil stand on the backline of the court. Then, from a point as high over his head as he can reach, I have him actually throw the racquet into or over the net in the direction of his opponent's service court. It's amazing how quickly the swing develops, even if it is a little tough on the "beat-up" racquet frame.

Peculiarly enough, the toss gets most players into trouble in learning to serve. The swing and toss must be synchronized so they work together and the ball and racquet head arrive at the correct spot in the air simultaneously. It usually makes the beginner feel a little as if he were trying to pat his head with his right hand and rub his stomach with his left at the same time. Instinctively the pupil wants to toss the ball high in the air and then hit at it. This is the wrong approach. *It is wrong to hit at your toss—you should always toss at your swing.* By this I mean you should start your swing and then, as your racquet is coming up, toss the ball to the spot where the racquet will hit it easiest above your head.

The method of tossing high in the air and then hitting the ball, as it's falling, has several disadvantages. Even if we admit that you may be able to time your swing, which is most difficult even for an expert, the method is poor:

1. It destroys the co-ordinated rhythm of arms and swing of racquet so necessary for control.

2. It is very tempting to look away from the ball when it is in the air so long. The instinctive desire is to glance at the opponent's court to see where you are going to hit the ball.

3. The wind may blow the ball off line, or the toss itself may lack direction, both of which are absolutely fatal to this type service.

Its only advantage lies in the time it allows to take a tremendous swing, but such a swing is not needed if you control your racquet head.

By using the proper method, starting the swing and then tossing to the racquet:

1. You gain surprise, since the ball is in the air so short a time that your opponent can't anticipate just when it will be hit.

2. You gain control, because the toss has less time to deflect and a shorter distance to go until hit.

3. You attain perfect rhythm, since the toss arm and the racquet arm go up together and keep the body balanced and ready to hit as hard or as easily as wished.

There are several common errors of service that I want to discuss before the stroke itself. We all know the fellow who winds up and whales the stuffing out of his first service, putting it in about once out of every thousand times, and then follows with an absolute lolly-pop that just pleads to be murdered. This man is all wet. Neither serve is worth the powder and shot to blow it up, and both should be forgotten.

Both first and second serves should be hit with the same general style of delivery and pace. The first should be hit as hard as you can control, well enough to put about two out of five in the court. The second should be hit as hard as you know will surely put it in. There is no excuse for serving double faults. It is the unforgivable tennis crime. Any player should be able to learn to hit a service so he can put at least 85 per cent of his services in play, and if he does, he will eliminate double faults, or reduce them to one or two a match.

There is another player who must be called to your attention as an eyesore on the tennis court. That is the windmill contortionist. How often have you seen him? He tosses the ball about fifteen feet in the air with mighty flailings of the racquet, one foot twists around his neck, his back bends, and then, as the ball falls to the level of his nose, he gently pushes it across the net. All his tremendous physical gyrations have been wasted. No part of his weight has gone into his serve.

Do not reach too high to serve, since by doing so you injure the rhythm of your swing and probably pull out your shirttail, but above all, do not let the ball fall so low that all you can do is push it over. Take the happy medium. Service should be hit at a point as high as you can *comfortably* reach. It should be hit with a full arm swing but without violent physical effort or unnecessary racquet waving. Keep your backswing simple and free, and without affectation.

The position, both as regards the place to stand behind the baseline and the actual stance of the feet, is the same for all three services. Personally, I advocate serving from a position about four feet to one side of the middle of the court, which will allow you to hit practically straight down the center line of the service court, and also give you plenty of chance to play the angle if desired. Place the feet with the left toe making about a 45-degree angle to the backline, the right one comfortably behind it, and the weight about evenly divided. Thereafter, until the ball is actually hit, do not move the left foot at all, and if the right one moves at all, just lift it, but do not swing it forward (except as noted in the American Twist explanation given below). One hears much about the Footfault Rule, and the prevalence of footfaulting among modern players. There is no need to footfault and it is usually the result of carelessness.

Footfaults most common are:

1. Stepping on the backline of the court.

2. Swinging a foot across the line before the ball is struck.

3. Jumping in the air so both feet leave the ground, even if behind the line.

4. Walking up to the line and serving without coming to a complete stop before commencing to serve.

To serve legally, stop and stand about three inches behind the backline and within the side and middle lines (if continued). Then keep *one foot* on the ground and *both* behind the line until the ball is hit. Once the ball is hit by the racquet, you can do anything with your feet. When you are serving, do not forget the courtesy due your opponent. Be sure he is ready to receive before you serve. The rules provide that he need not play your service unless he is ready, but often a player will hesitate to say "Not ready" and will miss a shot, because he is not quite set. The walking service or the hurried first ball is the usual offense. The easy and gracious way to stop these faults is, when you have come to your position and are ready to serve, to stop and take a look at your opponent to see if he is set. He will appreciate it.

Now for the actual mechanics of the three services. For all three, the Continental or Eastern Service grip, previously described on page 37, is used. It is shown again here, front view and back view.

Starting position

*Toss slightly
to right and
forward of head*

*Eye still on
ball as racquet
meets it*

A. The Slice Service. Having taken the position near the center of the baseline indicated previously, glance at your opponent's court to get your final direction, then look at the ball in your left hand. Let the racquet swing slowly back to the right of the body and then up to the right of the head and above it. Much of your weight has now gone back on your right foot. As the racquet starts up, start the left hand, holding the ball, up with it, and from a point about shoulder-high toss the ball to a point as high as the racquet will comfortably reach, slightly to the right of the head and about eight inches forward, toward the net. As your weight flows forward onto your left foot, throw the flat face of the racquet against the ball, meeting it on the upper right surface, and keep your eye fixed on the ball as you hit it. Do not look down at your opponent's court

*Follow-through
toward opponent's
service court*

*Note diagonal swing
of racquet head*

until the ball is hit. Having hit the ball, make the racquet head keep traveling directly at your opponent's service court. The racquet head carries directly through to the very end of the swing, ending below the waist on the left of the body. This will impart a spin, like a pitcher's out-drop curve, that will cause the ball to curve and bounce to your left (your opponent's right). Do not feel your job is done when the ball is struck, and let your arm sag and your swing collapse. Rather feel that the racquet head is going after the ball into your opponent's court.

45

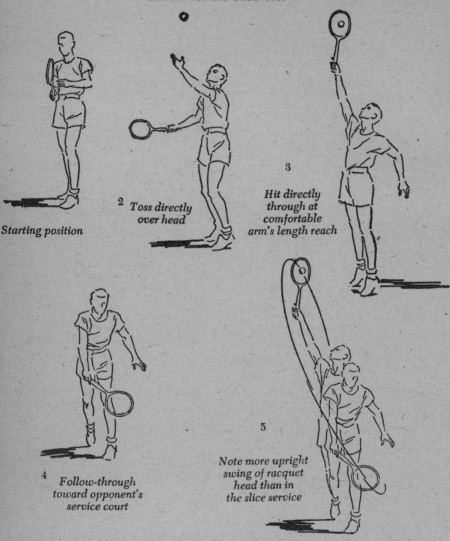

1
Starting position

2 *Toss directly over head*

3 *Hit directly through at comfortable arm's length reach*

4 *Follow-through toward opponent's service court*

5 *Note more upright swing of racquet head than in the slice service*

B. The Cannonball or Flat Serve. This is hit identically as described for the slice except that the ball is tossed directly over the head, and the racquet head meets the ball on the upper back surface, and hits directly through it. The so-called Cannonball is really nothing but a slice service with no slice.

Starting position

*Toss to left
of head—back
arched*

*Racquet head
comes up to
meet ball's
lower left
surface*

C. The American Twist. Here the stance is the same, but the back-swing carries the racquet head behind the back, which is bent. The ball is tossed to the left of the head and on a line parallel with it as regards the net. Keep the eye fixed on it. The racquet head comes from below, meets the ball on the lower left surface, hits up and over it with a distinct wrist "kick," and ends on the right of the body. In order to keep one's balance, the right leg comes up just about at the time the ball is met, and is extended in front of the body, following the line of the racquet, during the hitting-up-and-over part of the swing. The service curves from your right to left in

47

*Hitting up and
over—right leg
extended for
balance*

*Follow-through
with racquet
finishing on
right of body*

*Note that swing is
almost at a right angle
to direction of service*

the air but reverses on the bounce and goes from left to right or to your opponent's backhand. This service should be the last to be learned, and it can be mastered only by hard practice. It is slow and high, and the bound is high. It is a good second service, and is also excellent in doubles to allow the server to follow in to the net.

48

One often hears much of the various trick services like the Reverse, the Underhand Cut, etc. Personally I do not consider them of any real value, only as amusements. They do not confuse any player who knows his business, and I strongly urge young players to let them severely alone.

The way to use service, once it is learned, is almost a book in itself, but at least I can point out a few generalities that will help you to understand the tremendous advantage that a good service should give to a player. Few services can be hit hard enough to win outright by speed alone. Placement, deception, and surprise are the elements that really make service valuable.

Players get too set in their attitude toward their service. They are apt either to decide it is all an attack and hit the ball much too hard for safety or control, on both first and second delivery, or decide it is just a means to start the point and merely hit the ball in court, with too little speed or direction. Actually, service should always be used to place your opponent on the defensive, but there are many more ways to do it than by trying to blast him off the court with speed. I believe that one's total sum of service should consist of almost equal proportions of speed, spin, and direction, in the attempt to keep an opponent on the defensive, but these proportions should vary with each individual serve. One of the greatest fallacies in tennis is the belief that a very fast service is hard to return just because of its speed. Actually, the faster a service is, the easier it is to turn that speed back at the server if you can reach it to get your racquet face against it. The great French stars Henri Cochet and René Lacoste proved it, and such players as Bryan Grant, Jr., Clifford Sutter, Bobby Riggs, and Frank Parker have confirmed it in later years. The very fast service, to be really effective, must also have controlled direction. It is not Kramer's, Kovacs', and Gonzales' speed of service alone that wins aces for them, but rather their ability to put that speed into the corners of their opponents' service court.

The first requisite of a good server is control that allows him to put the ball on his opponent's forehand or backhand at will. The second thing is a sufficient amount of spin or twist to control the ball in the air, and cause it to bounce to the desired place. Finally, I believe in a sound medium pace, hard enough to prevent the receiver from attacking the serve, but not so hard as to tune up the opponent so there is no element of surprise left when you hit with great speed at times. The really fine server is the man who consistently varies spin, speed, and direction with each delivery. Most players get into a rut in serving. The great majority of players will serve a cross-court slice to the forehand in the right or number 1 court, and attempt to hit to the backhand in the left or number 2 court. They will do the same thing, game after game, set after set, so their opponent can practically stand in front of the coming delivery and not move. These players also always hit the first serve hard, and the second less hard. It is automatic, and not in any way due to intelligent thought. They throw away at least half the value of their service, no matter how good an actual stroke it may be. It would be far better if they divided the direction, perhaps 60 per cent to the forehand and 40 per cent to the backhand in the right, or number 1 court, and 40 per cent to the forehand and 60 per cent to the backhand in the left or number 2 court. Let these figures, too, be flexible so that they may vary to 70—30 per cent or down to 50—50 per cent. Remember the lowest place in the net is the center strap, which is three feet high, so if you are trying for an ace by speed alone, hit straight down the center line in either court. If you are attempting to ace a man with a sharp-angle serve in either court, it is done by subtlety of disguised direction of a slow delivery coupled with spin. Sheer speed won't work, since the net is so high at the sides that a sharp-angled hard-hit ball will go out if it clears the net. Do not start out serving to the limit of your ability at the beginning of a match. First, your arm is not yet warmed up and you may hurt it. Second, you will have no reserve left to call upon at the critical moments and climax of each set, when, above all, you should make service an attacking weapon that will still have an element of surprise left in it. The more critical the point, the greater care you should take in service. Above all, do not hurry your delivery. Never allow fear of error or nervousness to cause you to shorten your service swing, or cramp your style, for that will actually produce error. Do not waste your first service just because you have another coming if you miss. The amount of energy that can be wasted by hitting faults on the first service may be just enough to cost you victory at the end in a long, bitterly fought match.

There is another very important reason why you should concentrate on putting your first service in, even if it is not quite as severe as you might wish. Your opponent subconsciously expects you to waste a first service and is not quite set for it, whereas if you miss, he knows you must hit the second in, and is waiting and set to attack it. Above all, if you have run your opponent so far on the preceding point that he is winded, put that first ball in slow and safe. He will miss it many times from sheer fatigue and lack of concentration. Always seek to disguise direction so as to keep your opponent guessing on which side he must receive the ball. If you catch him on the wrong foot, you will often force an error with a comparatively weak service. Only if you are coming to the net behind service in singles are power, speed, and depth imperative. I do not believe anyone should continuously rush the net behind service, since I am convinced that against a first-class ground stroke the physical toll is too great and must fail in the end. The two greatest consistent net rushers behind service in the history of tennis were Jean Borotra and Vincent Richards, both of whom always met defeat in their important matches at the hands of such ground-stroke players as René Lacoste, Henri Cochet, William M. Johnston, and myself. On the other hand, I believe that every player should go in to the net behind service enough to keep the threat of it always in his opponent's mind. I think it is often an excellent idea to go in behind service at the climax of a match. Once more, intelligent variation is the thing. Keep your style mixed, varying speed, spin, and controlled direction, and your opponent will be muddled. Service should always be an asset and never a liability to the server.

Service, above all other shots, is a matter of practice, practice, and then more practice. As long as a player plays tennis he would do well to take a little time off once in a while, get a few dozen balls, and go out and practice service. The beginner should practice to get the right swing and just try to hit the ball into the correct court. As he improves he should start to work on direction. He should mark out a series of squares, eight by eight feet, along the service lines of the service courts, and try to hit into them. Then he should start hitting for the center line and the sideline, first one court and then the other, always with slow or medium pace. Only after he can put the ball within a few feet of his target better than 60 per cent of the time should he try to get great power. I advocate to my pupils who have advanced to the last stage that, even during tournament play, they take fifteen minutes a day, twice a week, to practice service. Remember that in service you and you alone are entirely responsible for the stroke and its result. It is the only shot in tennis in which you are not affected by your opponent's shot. Therefore, the perfect grooving of your muscular movements is the determining factor in your ability. Practice and practice alone will groove your muscles to respond as you wish to the call of your mind. When you turn to the other strokes in tennis you have not only to handle your own muscular movements and use your own brain to direct your shots, but you are brought into direct conflict with your opponent's mind and muscle through the medium of his shots. Therefore, your problems are more complex than in service.

CHAPTER 8

The Drive

WE WILL NOW take up the key stroke of tennis, on which all sound tennis games are, or should be, built.

The drive, on both wings, is the most important single stroke in tennis. It is played probably twice as often as all the other strokes combined. It is the key to all back-court games, and since a player must make at least one ground stroke before he can volley, you can see that ground strokes will always be more important than the net game. The drive is the only shot in tennis which is equally important in attack and defense. It can be used to win points outright by blasting speed or subtle placement, and it can also be used to keep the ball going back when you are being attacked by your opponent. It is capable of wider range of speed and angle than any other shot. Therefore, the wise student will learn to hit a drive first of all shots, and will strive to make it as sound and solid as practice will produce. A great many players will work hours to learn a backhand drive under able coaching but will be satisfied with almost any sort of natural poke on the forehand. There are few good forehands in tennis today. Actually, the forehand is more important than the backhand because it is, or should be, used more often. The basic method of hitting either drive is the same in attack and defense. It is only in the power of the swing of the racquet head and the direction of the stroke that the difference is to be found. Do not try to develop one type of drive in defense and another in attack—one way to hit cross-court and another to hit straight—because by so doing you will fail to have the ability to go from one to the other with no indication of what you intend to play.

The secret of a sound drive lies in the early preparation of the shot and the placing of the feet in correct position to keep your body sideways to the net, your rear end out of the way of the ball, and the weight moving forward with the stroke.

On all drives, no matter how high or low the point of contact with the ball may be, the head of the racquet must be dropped below the line of your shot. At the moment of hitting the ball, the racquet face should meet the lower outside surface of the ball with a slightly upward and definitely forward motion, and continue to the very end of the full arm swing.

Do not turn the racquet face over the ball with your wrist, or "lift up" across the ball, to impart topspin. The fact that you have hit slightly up on the ball with the flat racquet face, and followed through, will give you all the tendency to topspin that you need. Do not attempt to gain direction by "hooking" or twisting your drive. Let the flat face of your racquet go directly at the place you want the ball to go.

To drive cross-court from your right to left, lean a shade forward, letting the weight definitely go out on the left foot before the ball is struck, and meet the ball on a line with the left hip, or, in terms of time, hit it early.

To hit straight, or even from your number 2 court off to your right, keep your weight evenly divided between your feet and let the ball come back to a line with your belt buckle before you meet it, or, in terms of time, hit it late.

All drives should be hit waist-high! If the bound of the ball is too high to take it waist-high where you are standing, pick up your carcass and get in position where you can. Either move in and meet it waist-high as it comes up, which is dangerous even for experts and is used only in attack by them, or take the better and safer course and move back, letting the ball cross the top of the bound, and, as it falls to the waist, hit it. Should the bound of the ball be so low that it never rises to your waist, then you must bend your knees and take your waist down to the ball, but still hit it waist-high. Do not stand up like a cigar store Indian to these low shots and then use the shovel shot. It is no good.

Body sideways—racquet head back and ready below line of shot

Weight flows forward—eye fixed on ball

THE MECHANICS OF THE FOREHAND DRIVE

1. As the ball approaches, drop the racquet head down and back, behind the body.

2. Step across directly toward the right sideline with the left foot so your rear end is turned away from the ball.

3. Allow the weight to go forward toward the left foot, passing on it just before or just as you hit the ball.

4. With the eye never leaving the ball until you actually hit it, swing the racquet head around the body so the flat face of the racquet, with the short strings up and down, meets the ball on the lower right rear surface (away from you) and, with a *stiff wrist* and *firm grip* on the racquet, swing directly through, continuing the swing until the racquet head has traveled around your body and ends on your left with its opposite face turned to your opponent's court.

Follow-through around body—don't check swing after impact

Note completion of swing slightly upward and definitely forward

Few players realize that the follow-through is the thing that controls the drive. The reason so many players balloon shots into the backstop is that they swing into the ball, and as soon as they hit it they stop the racquet. The ball, with no spin to take hold of it, goes "poof" into the air. Timidity, fear of error, often stops a player from finishing his follow-through and results in the very thing he fears, whereas if he had had the courage to hit the ball and follow through, he would have made his shot. Never hit a drive without completing the arc of your swing, and that is just as true of the slowest, easiest shot as it is of the hardest. Indecision will ruin any shot. Make up your mind, and then play the ball with definiteness and decision to the very end of your swing.

*Body sideways—
back slightly
bent*

*Ball met on line
of front hip or
slightly forward of it*

THE BACKHAND DRIVE

Everything I pointed out in "The Mechanics of the Forehand Drive" is equally correct for the backhand if you substitute "right" for "left" and vice versa. You step over with the right foot directly toward the *left* sideline, let the weight pass on to the *right* foot, and meet the ball on its lower *left* surface. The one great difference in the backhand lies in the point where the racquet face contacts the ball. All forehands are hit directly in front of the body in a space between the lines of the front (or left) hip and the back (or right) hip. (Remember that the player is standing sideways.) On the backhand, the ball should be met sooner, that is, nearer the net. The latest point to hit a backhand drive is the line of the front (or right) hip, and from there to a point about two feet forward of the hip will produce the best results. The earlier you meet the ball, the sharper cross-court will your shot go. The reason for swinging soon is easily seen, since if you allow the ball to get on a line with the body, the arm must swing

57

back against the body, and at the moment of hitting it is still cramped in its swing. The secret of a good backhand lies in the freedom of the swing and the long follow-through. Most players have a tendency to poke at a backhand, so there is little control or power to the shot.

Long follow-through
towards opponent's
court

As in the forehand drive,
the swing is slightly upward
and definitely forward

The main uses of the drive are:

1. To return service (both attack and defense).
2. To make passing shots against the net player (attack).
3. To advance to the net behind a forcing shot (attack).
4. To hit clean winners (attack).
5. To open your opponent's court and maneuver him out of position (subtle attack).
6. To get yourself out of trouble when you are forced into bad position (defense).

From these six uses you can see that the drive is primarily an attacking shot but not necessarily so and, if used as an attack, is very often not an outright winner but is used to build up the point for a winner—often from the net. Therefore, it should carry a fairly high average pace but only at times should it be slugged with full power. Too many modern players have only one drive, and that is at the top of their power. The sound average-pace drive, and the slow drive with its insidious weapon of variation, are the greatest losses of tennis today, and they must be regained.

Let us discuss each of the six uses of the drive separately in greater detail:

1. **To Return Service.** About 80 per cent of all services received are capable of being driven back at the server. Of this percentage, only 10 per cent are capable of being hit for outright winners by the receiver. About half of the remaining 70 per cent can be attacked and about half defended with the drive. The receiver who will concentrate on getting service into play puts his opponent under a tremendous pressure. Nothing is so discouraging to a player as to see his good attacking service come back deep into the middle of the court, making him start all over again. The first and most valuable use of the drive is successfully to defend against a service. Do not try to do too much with your first return of service. Be content to put the ball in play, fairly deep into your opponent's court, but with a wide margin of safety. So many players try to paste every service return, and all they produce is a deluge of their own errors. Only if a server is coming in behind his service is there much reason to try to do anything very special with a service return. Then you must be very definite, but rather than take an unnecessary chance in trying to win outright, I advocate hitting a slow, low drive that gives the server a volley that he cannot do much with, and then hit out for your passing shot off his volley. In hitting a service return, make it definitely cross-court or definitely straight, but allow yourself plenty of margin of safety. Do not hit for a line, since if you draw it so fine, you will make too many unnecessary errors. Hit your drive hard enough so that it will not sit up, but there is no need to use anything above good average speed. Should the server be careless enough to hit a weak serve that bounds up where you like it, then do not hesitate, but wade in and hit hard for a winner. These chances are few and far between, and you should not try for them off good attacking serves. You should give most returns of

service plenty of room to clear the net. Off a service, when the server stays back on the baseline, the return drive should be not less than a foot nor more than three feet above the net. In the event that the server comes in, then the drive should never be higher than a foot above the net and the closer to the net cord the better, if you do not draw it too fine. Better to be too high and give your opponent a volley, than too low and give him the point by an error. A shot that clears the net always has a chance, but a shot into the net is dead and gone.

2. **To Make Passing Shots.** The drive is always the best passing shot in tennis. This is because it has a tendency to drop early because of its natural top spin. It is the shot that is capable of the widest range of speed and pace with the least sacrifice of control. Remember that when you hit for a passing shot, you hit for the point and, therefore, there must be complete decision and finality about the stroke. Passing shots should never be hit at the same average pace used in defense or in maneuvering. They should definitely be hit harder, or much slower. The slow, angled passing shot, which in modern tennis has been badly overlooked during the past decade, is the most valuable of all passing shots because:

a. It can be played into the widest reaches of your opponent's court.

b. Its direction is far easier to disguise than a hard shot, since it takes much less obvious physical preparation.

c. Even if it does not win outright, it is very difficult to volley. It forces the net player to put all the speed on the volley himself, a difficult thing to do.

The passing drive is hit off service or from deep in the court in the vast majority of cases. This means it must be a very hard hit shot, because of the distance it must travel before it can pass the net player, who has plenty of time to move to a slow shot.

If the fast passing shot is hit cross-court, it also requires a fairly sharp angle to win. It is better to attempt a slow deceptively drop-ping drive as your cross-court passing shot. This will force the net player to volley it if he reaches it, and give you another chance to pass him. Only by completely outguessing the net player in direc-tion will a slow, angle drive win outright from the baseline.

However, on short drives taken inside the service line, the soft, slow passing shot is much more effective than the hard hit drive, since a hard shot if it crosses the net will often go out. Only if the bound of the short shot is above the level of the net, so it can be driven down, is it good to slug a short shot. The thing that so many players forget in attempting to hit hard passing drives off short shots is that they are probably twenty feet into their own court, and that twenty feet is gone. It is not tacked on the back or sides of their opponent's court. If you must hit the ball hard in these instances, the straight drive is usually the best passing shot.

Whenever you go out for a passing shot with a drive, mentally and physically move in with your shot. If you have a very small space to hit through, and very little time to do it in, then actually move in, meeting the ball on the rising bounce, and go all out for your point. If you have plenty of time, take it. Approach your shot with your racquet back and your decision made. Move in, glide in to the ball, and hit it decisively as it falls to your waist *without look-ing at either your opponent or the hole at which you are hitting*. By keeping your eye on the ball, you give almost no indication of where your shot is going. Most net players get their advance in-formation concerning your shot from your glance at the place you intend to hit, just before you hit there. Make the net player guess, and make your shot definite, determined, and either really hard or really slow.

The drive should be used also to give you the opening for your passing shot. A net player hits an attacking shot and starts in to the net. Do not attempt to pass him off his attacking shot, but play a low, medium-paced, short drive that makes him reach, and forces him to volley up. His defensive volley off such a shot will usually be high and short. Then, move in on the ball and go all out for a clean winning passing shot. I do not mean that you must never attempt to pass the advancing net player off his attacking shot. There are exceptions to all rules. But do it seldom, and when you do, hit hard, very hard and low, so there is no answer to your shot if it's successful. Win or lose the point with your drive, if you try to pass in that way. The great majority of points against the net player's advance should be played as I first described—with the slow defensive drive.

The logical follow-up to how to meet a net player with a drive is how to use the drive yourself in reverse circumstances.

3. **To Advance to the Net behind a Forcing Shot.** Here is the one place that the drive taken on the rising bounce is of great value, although it can be overdone and is not always the logical shot to play. The only advantage of the rising bounce drive is that you are nearer to the net when you hit it than if you wait for the ball to reach the top of its bound and fall to your waist level. Therefore, you reach the net sooner, which gives your opponent less time to get his return by you before you have net position. Against this advantage, which is a big one, is the greatly increased danger of error, owing to the difficulty of timing a rising bounce shot. The two best rising bounce players in tennis history, F. J. Perry and Henri Cochet, never played more than 40 per cent of their drives on the rise, but almost all the ones they did play were used in advancing to the net. Personally, I prefer the method of waiting for a midcourt shot from my opponent, which I can move in on and play moving forward as the ball is falling, rather than take a rising bound off a deep shot and attempt to go in behind it. There is too great a chance for error in the latter case. The advancing drive off either the forehand or backhand must have three important features to be effective:

a. It must have depth, hitting within at least six feet of the backline.

b. It must have power—at least enough so that it will not pop up and give your opponent a chance to attack.

c. It must go into a corner or side of the court, so your opponent is forced to play his defensive shot running.

Depth, pace, and direction—never go to the net behind a shot that does not have all three of these qualities.

Do not attempt to win outright with the drive that you are following to the net. If you do, you overhit. There is no need to take an unnecessary risk, because the shot is merely intended to force a weak return that you will then kill at the net. All advancing shots should be accompanied by one fixed quality in your mind and body. Advance! Move in with the ball as you hit it. Do not make the mistake of moving in with your body and leaving your racquet behind you so you hit the ball late. Lean in and reach forward to the ball and *follow* your shot. Vary the direction of your advancing shot. Too many players have only one direction in which they hit when preparing an advance to the net. Usually it is to the opponent's backhand, and it's made from the center of the court or from the side with a straight shot down the line. They either forget their opponent's forehand corner, or are afraid to go in against the forehand. Actually, you should have no favorite method of advance. You should go in with equal confidence and equally often against the forehand or backhand behind cross-court or straight shots, whenever the logical chance to attack is there. Keep your opponent guessing which way you'll go in. Once more, variation and intelligence should always govern your choice of advancing shots.

Out of the advancing shot comes the next step of the drive, which shows it as seen too often today.

4. **To Hit Clean Winners.** Here you find the most prevalent use of the drive in modern tennis; at least that is the intention behind the wild swattings that go on in returning service and at every other possible chance. There is such a desire to hit clean winners every time that many players, with basically sound drives, throw away most of what they have in their desire to win spectacularly outright. That is one of the greatest weaknesses of our present National

Champion, Richard Gonzales. He is supposed to have had bad ground strokes. I disagree with this diagnosis. I think the general method of stroke production of both his forehand and backhand drives, while not ideal, is far better than that of most of the present group, but he attempts to hit so many outright winners that he seldom cashes in on his potential stroke production soundness.

There are only three situations in which to go all out for clean winners with a drive:

a. On any weak service, a weak mid-court shot opens your opponent's court so that speed plus fair direction will win. When that shot is offered you, then haul off and hit it flat with the full power of your swing. Be certain that it wins or loses right there. The shot is played to end the point. Off service in the number 1 or right court, the best clean winner is to wade in and paste it cross-court into your opponent's forehand corner. In this shot you can hit around the ball and gain more control with great speed than you would have hitting down the straight line. Also, you have more room and a lower net to cross. (The number 2 or left court offers no logical preference for a clean winner. You must make your own shot, since to hit your forehand from there you usually have to run around your backhand.)

b. The second type of outright winner I have already discussed. It is the passing shot against the incoming net man.

c. The third is the "neck or nothing" shot, when you are placed at a hopeless disadvantage, thrown far out of court with no hope of getting back in position. On such a shot, take every possible chance, since you have everything to win and nothing to lose. You are beaten anyway unless you pull off a winner, so hit it as hard as you can, and for the most daring place you can think of. Try for a line at a time like this and give it all you have.

You can see from these three situations that you always take a chance when you hit for clean winners. Obviously, your percentage of errors on such occasions will be far too high to stand up over a long period of time. Therefore, when you do go for your winner, be very careful to pick a time when it will either pay you greatly if you pull it off or it can do you no harm if you fail, since you are already in trouble. When you are thinking about the thrill of going after winners, just calm yourself by remembering that tennis matches are always lost on errors and never won by placements. Do not be carried away by the present trend to go out for clean winners all the time. Play the percentage shot, which will pay off in the end. Far better than attempting to hit for winners continuously and piling up a tremendous number of errors is to use the drive intelligently.

5. **To Open Your Opponent's Court and Maneuver Him out of Position.** Here one finds the exact reverse of the rules for use of the drive for clean winners. In using the drive as an opening or maneuvering shot, you should never take an unnecessary chance; always allow a wide margin of safety over the net and a reasonable one to the side- and backlines. This drive should always carry good average pace, fast enough to insure that your opponent must run to reach it, but not so fast as to risk error or even to win outright. You use the medium-pace drive to tire your opponent and to force errors. I am a great believer in setting a definite rhythm to a point of this type and holding it until you have your opening. Only when the opening is clearly made and the chance to win outright is there do you lift the pace to great speed or drop it to a soft, slow drive. The most effective way to open your opponent's court is to hit alternately to the forehand and backhand, attempting to widen the angle with each drive until you see that the distance is sufficiently great to allow for the winner. Once you have swung your opponent wide enough so that he is chasing back and forth, then comes the killing drive. There are four ways to win the point—two of them at great speed, two of them with slow, soft drives. The best way to win with speed is to hit to the farthest corner of the court on the opposite side—the hard, deep cross-court. The fast, deep, straight drive is not so good since, if your opponent can stop and turn, he will probably reach it. On the other hand, the best soft, slow drive for the winner

is the short, straight one, for on that your opponent must not only stop but turn and run forward as well. The slow, sharply angled cross-court is not quite so good, since your opponent is already moving across the court and may be able to come forward in time to reach it.

Above all, remember that no matter how regular you may be in your method of opening your opponent's court by the corner-to-corner method, you must vary your kill shot, or your opponent will be set for it. It does not matter if he knows you are going to run him back and forth across the court. There is nothing much he can do to prevent it, if you keep your depth and direction but do not advertise how you are going to make your kill by using the same shot all the time.

6. **To Get Yourself Out of Trouble.** This is the defensive drive. Let us consider the position of the player who is being run mercilessly from corner to corner. What can he do to save himself? The usual method of chasing the shot down and hitting it back at sound average pace into the center of the other court gets you nothing more than a chase into the other corner of your court. You can, of course, take a chance and slug it, but the percentage of errors is too high to pay off. There is only one thing left, if you use a drive, and that is to take as much pace off your shot as you can and hit a high, slow floater back deep into your opponent's court. This type shot will:

a. Give you time to regain position in your court by the time your opponent hits the ball, which at once cuts down your run.

b. By taking the speed and pace out of the point and floating the shot, make your opponent wait, break the rhythm of the point, and change his timing.

This shot makes him think and is apt to make him hit his next shot tentatively. He must put the pace back into the point if he wishes to attack, always difficult off soft shots, and if he does not, then your chance has come. If he plays a tentative slow shot in return, move in on it and, without attempting to slug it, hit it decisively and start your own attack. Either move him from corner to corner or, if his shot is really weak, go in to the net behind a drive. By that one previous floating defensive slow drive, you have turned the entire complexion of the point from defense to a situation where you can attack. This defensive drive should not be overplayed, and in most cases, as will be seen later, the better change of pace is a slice or chop, but as a variation in getting out of real difficulty, the high, slow, floating drive is the greatest defense I know. A lob high in the air will not do the same thing, as you will learn later when the lob is discussed. The slow floating drive alone will produce the desired result. It is hit exactly like the average pace, but with almost a slow-motion racquet head swing.

Do not hesitate to use your backhand drive for attack as well as defense. Too many players have a complex about hitting aggressively off their backhand. They will pass up many opportunities to hit mid-court shots on the backhand for winners, or run around them to take them on the forehand and, by so doing, get out of position. Do not develop one side at the expense of the other. It is just as easy to hit a ball soundly on one side as on the other if you are willing to do the work to learn how, and if you are willing to practice to master the technique. A well-rounded game is a great asset, and mastery of it can be acquired only by hours of work.

Never underestimate the value of the drive. If a player could have only one shot, a drive would carry him the furthest. Since tennis was an infant, this has been true. From A. W. Gore of England in the 1890's, through Francis T. Hunter with his crushing forehand, to Donald Budge and his miraculous backhand, it has held true. Only during the past decade, when the net game has been overemphasized and many incompetent coaches have been advising our young players, has the drive fallen below its proper place in popular esteem. As it fell, so fell the standard of the game. As it comes back, so will the standard come back with it.

CHAPTER 9

The Chop and the Slice

PASSING FROM the drive to the only other ground strokes of major importance, we now take up the chop stroke and the slice shot. The only difference between the two is in the angle made by the racquet head's hitting plane and the flight of the ball. In a chop, the angle made by the racquet head's hitting plane and the flight of the ball *if extended past the point of contact* is greater than 45 degrees.

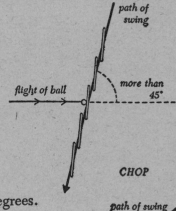

In a slice, that angle is less than 45 degrees.

Since the technique of play is almost the same for both strokes, in this chapter I'll use both terms indiscriminately, but it is my personal opinion that almost all such shots should be slices, and not chops.

*Racquet making angle
with arm—racquet
head above line of shot*

*Stroking down and
through ball—
slightly loosened
wrist imparts backspin*

In chopping or slicing, there should be a slight tendency to slant the racquet head backward, but do not exaggerate this, or you will "pop" the ball up in the air. The backspin on the ball, which comes from hitting down and under it, gives the ball a tendency to rise, so the added lift of trajectory is not needed, and it leads to error.

Whereas a drive is always hit through and up, with a tendency toward topspin, a slice is always hit through and down, with a tendency toward backspin. Just as a drive will hit and hop forward, owing to the forward motion of its spin, the slice, with its reverse rotation, has a tendency to stop and "drag" in its bound. The drive has a higher bound than a chop, from the same line of flight. It has been pointed out that the drive is an attacking shot that under certain conditions can be used in defense. The slice is essentially a defensive stroke that in a few circumstances can be used in attack, and that attack is always one of subtle deception and finesse, never of sheer speed. The mechanics of the slice are very simple and much more flexible than those of the drive, because the wrist plays so great a part in the stroke. Although footwork is still important, if it isn't perfect it does not completely ruin the shot, as is true of the drive.

*Follow-through
completely without
too much wrist*

*Swing is definitely
down—racquet face
only slightly
slanted back*

THE MECHANICS OF THE SLICE

1. The grip is the Eastern service or Continental grip (number 3), descibed on page 37. It does not change between the fore- and backhand.

2. The same footwork as on the drive, with the body turned sideways and the rear end turned out of the way by stepping across directly at the opposite sideline with the foot away from the ball, will produce the best results. However, owing to the use of the wrist in the actual swing, in marked contrast to the stiff wrist that must be used for drives, the feet need not be so definitely changed provided the weight is kept on the one closer to the ball.

3. Let the head of the racquet rise slightly above the wrist as it is taken back a short distance behind the body. This makes an angle between racquet and arm. Be sure the racquet head is slightly above the line of the proposed shot. Swing the racquet head directly into the ball from slightly above it, and let it travel on through to the end of its swing, aided by a loosened wrist that carries the racquet slightly *under* the ball and imparts a backspin to it. Be sure to follow through completely, and do not attempt to use too much wrist or the ball will float.

*Racquet making angle
with arm—racquet
head above line of shot*

*Ball met slightly
farther forward than
in forehand slice*

To hit a slice that travels from your right to your left (cross-court from number 1 court) hit the ball on the upper right surface. To hit from your left to your right (a backhand cross-court from number 2 court) hit the ball on the upper left surface. To hit straight, meet the ball at the back or slightly to the left of center.

The slice is definitely not a shot capable of great speed with control, since backspin, working against the air, causes the ball to rise and float. It is a shot that should either be hit on a straight trajectory or, if the bound is high enough, hit down, but it is not a shot on which to hit up. For this reason it is not a stroke to use on low, short shots.

The main uses of a slice are:

1. To vary pace on your opponent, mixing it in with a drive, and to take pace out of great speed and slow up the tempo of a point (defense).

2. To return great speed on service (defense).

3. To handle shots that catch you out of position, particularly shots that bound too high to drive (defense).

4. As an advancing shot behind which to go to the net (attack).

71

*Follow-through
completely without
too much wrist*

*Swing is definitely
down—racquet face
only slightly
slanted back*

Notice that three of its four greatest uses are defensive and only one is for attack. Even that one is not quite as good for regular use as a drive would be. Certainly the slice's greatest value to an intelligent player lies in the following uses:

1. To Vary Pace on Your Opponent By Mixing It with a Drive and to Take Pace out of Great Speed and Slow up Tempo. Almost all players like to get in a groove and play along mechanically. Even great players are like that, and unless their groove is broken they are almost unbeatable. Ellsworth Vines, Donald Budge, Welby Van Horn, Frank Parker, Carl Earn, Jack Kramer, Billy Talbert, Gardnar Mulloy, Pancho Gonzales, and Ted Schroeder all could hit a groove and, unless they could be broken out of it, would play flawless tennis. Yet, if they were once stopped, they often were unable ever again to find their groove during that particular match. The men who are the best upsetters of a groove player by cleverly mixing their game are Fred J. Perry and Bobby Riggs, both of whom stood supreme at their respective peaks. The insidious way that Riggs spoiled Budge's timing by alternating speed with slow, low ground strokes and amazing lobs so broke Budge's game that he could do nothing against Riggs from that time on. There is no one shot that can play so conspicuous a part in upsetting a man's game as the skillfully used slice when employed as a variation to the drive. Do not get me wrong. The slice alone, or even a topheavy proportion of slices over the drive, is not good. It is too slow and defensive, but mixed in the proper proportion with the drive it is a fine error producer. Its value also varies according to the court surface.

It is most valuable on clay, where its twist is very effective. The drag is greater, the bound lower and shorter. It is next most effective on grass. It is worth little on concrete, asphalt, or cement, where it bounds too high and is easy to hit, while on wood it is useless. However, since most of the important tennis is played on clay and grass, one must consider its value from those standpoints.

The chop should be used for somewhere between 20 and 40 per cent of ground strokes hit. Conversely, the drive will make up the other 80 to 60 per cent. If you are playing against a very hard hitter, increase your percentage of chops so as to slow up the pace. You can almost go to 50-50 per cent if your opponent finds trouble controlling his drive against the changing pace. Do not fall into the habit so many players have, of using just one type of shot throughout a point, even if you change the type on the next point. That is not mixing up your strokes. If you drive twice in a row in a point, slide in a chop, or if you start chopping, after two or three shift to a drive for a shot or two. Every time you change the spin and pace on your shots, you force your opponent to be very careful, and if his concentration has slackened, the change of spin and pace will make him miss. Nothing is more wearing on a player than having to wait out a spin shot and play it with care. It puts a great mental pressure on him which is just as tiring as his physical exertions. The longer a player is forced to dig up a deep slice into the corners, and then rouse himself to meet a solid offensive drive, the more he will feel the load of pressure. The effects of the chop or slice are cumulative. By that I mean it is easy to hit back in the first set, but it becomes a whale of an effort to dig it and ladle it back in the fourth. When mixing up a drive and a chop in the same point, keep a definite gap between the pace of the two. Hit the drive with full average pace, and then hit the chop with little power but plenty of depth and spin.

In some cases, your opponent is supplying the driving power. It is almost axiomatic that speed begets speed. Therefore, if you are playing a very hard hitter, he will thrive on your speed. The average hard hitter likes to exert his power off a solidly hit ball. On the other hand, he finds difficulty in starting speed against soft fluff. To slow up the tempo and reduce the pace whenever your opponent pastes a shot and stays back, hit a high floating chop, with a lot of backspin, that will hang in the air, drag off the ground, and bound low. The tendency of the hitter is to get overanxious and hit too soon, usually causing him to net his return. I found this method of slow chopped floaters particularly effective against such terrific drivers as Little Bill Johnston, Ellsworth Vines, Donald Budge, and players of that type. Naturally, if your opponent follows his driving attack with an advance to the net, the chop must be abandoned, since it is too slow and has too high a trajectory for a successful passing shot. But just so long as the hard driver stays back, the chop or slice is the ideal defense to break him up.

2. To Return Great Speed on Service. Everything that applies to the defense against the fast drive is true of the defense against the fast service. The advantages are even greater because the server must actually start the point all over if you have simply sliced and floated the ball back into his deep court. All his service advantage has been lost, and psychologically the pressure grows each time his attacking service comes back in this manner.

3. To Handle Shots That Catch You Out of Position—Particularly the Shoulder-high Bounce. In starting to move the wrong way for a shot, all players get caught on the wrong foot a reasonably large number times each set. In the case of the player who attempts to drive, the result is usually an error because he has not time (1) to get his feet in position, (2) to get his racquet head down and back, (3) to get his body out of his way. This is where the chop comes into play, with its short, high backswing and use of the wrist in the curtailed swing. The slice or chop can be played, even if the feet are wrong and the body in the way of a full swing, simply by lifting the racquet head and flicking it with the wrist against the ball. It is purely defensive, almost a reflex action to save being hit by the ball at times, but it can and will get the racquet head against the ball more quickly than any other shot, and it will at least keep the ball in play. Since the grip used need not be changed from forehand to backhand, this defense is equally easy on either side. Players are often caught in "no-man's-land" inside the backline by a high-bounding shot that they must return at a shoulder-high level. A few can hit a forehand drive there, but practically none a backhand drive. Any drive at that level is awkward and uncertain. This is another case where the chop, by its very nature—high racquet head and general downward swing—is ideal to handle the situation. It is the only sound answer to high-bounding American twist or kick service on the backhand, which causes so many players trouble. To hit that high bound, be sure your body is sideways, your rear end away from the ball, and that you are not crowding it. Then lift your racquet head, lean into the ball, meeting it on the *upper left surface*, and chop down and through it, being sure to follow through to the end of your swing.

The final use of the chop, and its only attacking use, is

4. As a Means to Advance to the Net. The same rules of direction, depth, and power hold true as those set forth previously for a drive in this situation. The chop behind which one advances to the net is the only chop or slice that should be hit hard. It might well be called a slice-drive, since its trajectory must be low, like a drive, and without the floating quality that marks the defensive slice. It should be used only in mid-court shots that bound at least as high as the waist. It is particularly effective for bounds up to the shoulders or head. Its greatest advantage lies in the fact that it can be hit from almost any position, and usually from a point closer in to the bounce of the ball than a drive, so the advance to the net is a shade faster. It also has the advantage of being hit with the same grip as the volley and smash, so there is no need to change grip for your first net shot. The drive, which has a distinct grip of its own, requires a shift to the volley grip.

Do not forget that:

1. The drive is the key stroke and the most important of all, since it is used in attack and defense.

2. The chop or slice is secondary in importance by itself, but is vital to defense and to the ability to vary your game.

No player is completely well rounded without both shots in his repertoire. A player is actually only as strong as his ground strokes, no matter how great his net game is, since only behind ground strokes can he reach the net.

CHAPTER 10

The Net Game: The Volley; The Overhead Smash

THE net game—the volley and overhead smash—represents the ultimate attack in tennis. It is the crushing offensive that either blasts an opponent off the court or wrecks itself by the very fury of its own attack. In that case it is likely to end in physical exhaustion, collapse, and futile effort. It is of primary importance in men's tennis but, while valuable, is not nearly so important in women's. This is due entirely to the physical factors. Most men can stand the strain of a net attack for three sets, and a big percentage can even go the long route of five sets, but very few women have the physical stamina to go to the net consistently for three hard sets.

No one can be a completely well-equipped player without an adequate net game, but once more I state emphatically, the net game is secondary to the ground game. After all, under the rules of tennis, there must be at least one ground stroke before a volley or smash can be played. It is the tremendous overemphasis on the net game today, with its resultant loss of good solid ground strokes, that is largely responsible for the deplorable state of junior tennis in the United States. However, no matter how strongly I feel that the drive and the slice must be brought back to their proper place in tennis, I must not make the mistake of underestimating the tremendous value of the net game in attack. The net is the ultimate goal of a player, once he decides to attack, and no matter how long he may have to defend or maneuver to get there, he must never lose sight of that fact. The point I want to make is that he cannot afford to go there carelessly, indiscriminately, or all the time. His advance to the net should always be made after careful, proper preparation when his opponent has been placed on the defensive, and when the chances of making a winning shot are better than fifty-fifty. He should never go to the net just because someone told him it should invariably be done. He should do it when his own intelligence directs it, because he has worked up his attack to that point. When you go to the net, you do it for one thing only: to win the point outright with a kill. Never defend at the net. Never give your opponent another chance after your first shot if you can help it, but if you do, the next shot must win or lose outright. The net game is Sudden Death. If you have any timidity, any fear of error, any thought of defending, stay away from that net. The very daring and audacity of the net attack is what makes the galleries love to watch it. No players had more gallery appeal than Jean Borotra and Vincent Richards, the two greatest net players of all time. It is the net rushing of Pancho Gonzales that has made him such a gallery pleaser. Only the daring and brilliance of the net games of Bobby Falkenberg, Jimmy Brink, and the others of their type give them fame and bring in the crowds to watch them, because they are not really first-class tennis players. The beauty and skill of the all-around games of Fred Perry, Don Budge, and Ellsworth Vines were lost sight of by most spectators, who saw only their crashing overheads or amazing volleys. I think one reason modern tennis carries such a tremendous overemphasis on the net game is that the young players like the howl of applause from the gallery that follows some particularly spectacular smash or volley. In the glow it gives them, they forget their dismal errors off the ground. Yet, to the expert eye, the subtle and clever games of such players as Riggs and Parker and the quieter moments of Budge and particularly Perry bring far more joy in the artistry displayed.

THE VOLLEY

The mechanics of the volley are identical on the forehand and on the backhand, with only the feet reversed.

1. The grip is the number 3 grip, the service or Continental as shown here.

2. The footwork is the same as for a ground stroke if there is time to accomplish the movement. The foot away from the ball steps directly across toward the opposite sideline, thus turning the body sideways to the net and the rear end away from the ball. In many cases a shot is coming directly at the volleyer, and in this case, step directly backward with the foot closest to the ball on the side you wish to play it. Swing that foot back and behind you toward the opposite sideline. This will produce the same result as above. Many times a shot comes so suddenly at a volleyer that there is no time to change the feet. If that happens, throw your weight on the foot closest to the ball, and lean forward.

3. Lift the racquet head above the wrist with a very short backswing. Move the racquet head forward into the line of flight of the oncoming ball, and meet it flat with a stiff wrist about six to ten inches closer to the net than the foremost line of your body. *Block the ball* directly to where you want it to go, and *above all, do not follow through*. The volley should gain its power from the opponent's shot, plus the solidity of your block and stiff wrist. This is for the ordinary volley. Later, I will mention an exception in the short drop volley.

4. The lower the shot you must volley, the more you must bend your knees, since on *all* volleys the *racquet head* should be *above the wrist* at the moment of meeting the ball. Do not attempt to hit through or drive any volley below the level of the head. Be content to let your racquet face make the angle, and gain the power from your opponent's shot. Volleys win by direction, placement, far more than they do by speed.

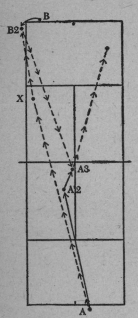

NET POSITION

Showing how the net player covers the court, and particularly the straight shot, by following the line of his own shot. *Solid line—movement of players; broken line—flight of ball.*

A serves. Ball bounces at X.

B, from position, moves to B2 and receives it, hitting it back down the center.

A followed in along the line of his shot and a little toward the center to A2. He is ready to go farther to his left in case B should try a passing shot down the sideline, but when he sees the ball hit, he moves farther toward center and volleys at A3 to the opposite side from B.

Continuing the situation:

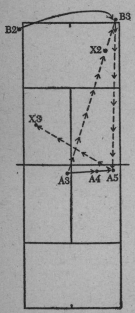

A's volley (from A3) bounces at X2.

Meanwhile B moves from B2 across and behind the ball, taking it at B3 and playing it straight down the sideline.

A has moved to A4 to cover the straight shot; he now takes another step to A5, and wins with a killing cross-court volley to X3.

If B had elected to try a cross-court drive himself on his last shot, it would have been very difficult to pass A and keep the ball in court, since, from A4, A can block off any return from B except a very sharply angled and perfectly stroked shot.

THE VOLLEY POSITION

The most decisive factor in the ability to volley lies in correct position. Almost equally important is the method of reaching that position. They are far from the same thing. I know many players who, once planted at the net in position, volley very well, but if they have to run in to position, they miss three quarters of their volleys. This is due, first, to their lack of preparation on the way, and, second, to their coming in on the wrong line. Such a player can volley on his partner's service in doubles, but not on his own, and he is always in trouble in singles. The correct volley position is six to ten feet from the net and about two to three feet to the center side of a straight line, drawn from the point your opponent is hitting his shot straight down your court parallel to the sidelines. There is nothing difficult about remembering that, but to reach it in time, and hold it, is a quite different thing. Let us take the situation where you have reached correct position, and see what you have to do to hold that position.

You make your first volley cross-court from your forehand, so that your opponent plays it at a point four feet inside his sideline. You were standing about halfway between the center line and the sideline on your right side when you hit your volley and about eight feet back from the net. Obviously you must change your position or get passed, since the whole backhand side of your court is open and the ball is over there. The point is, how far over do you go? Most players move into the middle of the court on the center line and think they are covering the court. They are wrong. The straight shot, which is the easiest passing shot, is still wide open. The correct move is well beyond the center line to a point about seven feet inside the left sideline and still about eight feet back from the net. By making this move, you have really covered the straight shot and can still cut off any cross-

81

court shot except an almost perfect one. If your opponent makes the perfect shot, give him full credit for it and don't worry about it. He won't do it often. Always play the percentage position, the position that can reach the majority of your opponent's attempts to pass.

At the net you seldom have more than two thirds of your court to cover. There is the straight third in front of the ball, and the middle third in front of a cross-court that an opponent can hit into with little risk. However, the remaining third, on the extreme side of the court away from the ball, is so difficult to hit into with a passing shot that clears the net that you can afford to give your opponent the few shots he will win with, in return for the greater number of errors he will make attempting to do so. Therefore, your position must always physically cover the straight shot, mentally you must be prepared for the middle third shot, and forget all about the very sharp-angle third.

To do this, in coming to the net from backcourt, always follow the line of your shot, but stay just to the center side of it. You move to position about halfway up the swing of a pendulum that has its apex at the baseline of your court, and the swinging end of the pendulum is your opponent. The greatest error the average player makes is thinking that he must cover his whole court as he comes in. The only time that is true is when the advancing shot is hit down the center of your opponent's court, since on that shot the passing shot angle is not difficult for him to make, and there is practically no reason for him to make an error. If you are coming in to the net, as I pointed out in connection with the advancing drive, don't hit down center but definitely hit into a corner of the court, or on a sharp angle. In so doing you at once can put out of your mind about one third of your court as territory you must cover.

When you make the advancing shot, move in along the line of your shot, steadily, but not so fast that you cannot turn or stop easily. Prepare to volley on the way in. Many players forget this most important point, and arrive with their racquets hanging. Actually, you should carry your racquet with head up in front of you, and reach forward to the ball to volley it. Too many players reach the position in time to volley but let the ball come too deep to them and volley it at the side of the body instead of before it has reached the body line. A late volley has a tendency to pop up in the air and carries no pace on the shot. Do not let the ball come to you, but go out with your racquet and meet it on its way.

There is another common error among volleyers: attempting to do too much with their first volley if they are caught too far back, and are not really at the net. They try to make a kill from mid-court and miss. The correct way to handle the advancing volley, played from mid-court, is to block it deep and continue into correct volleying position for the kill on the next shot. When I urged you to go out for your kill at once on the volley, I meant "at once" *after you are in correct position for it*. No shot you make has a good chance for a clean kill unless you are in a correct position. Many players make too great an attempt to volley short, slow, deceptive returns as they are coming in. They plunge at the ball, volley it off their shoestrings, and usually miss it or pop it weakly. If they used their heads, they would have stopped, let it bounce, and driven or chopped it deep and then moved into the volleying position. They probably were moving forward too fast and couldn't stop. Once more, let me urge you always to move so you keep your weight and balance under control. Do not rush, hurry, plunge around, and jump like a puppy just out of a lake and all full of the glow of well-being. Make every move tell, and make it for a definite purpose. There is too much tennis played today that has no thought behind it or directing it, and nowhere is that more true than in the advance to the net. When you watch such players as Henri Cochet, Fred Perry, Donald Budge, and Bobby Riggs go in to volley, you feel that they practically walk into position. You get no impression of scurrying, scrambling, or digging, as you do from players like Bobby Falkenberg, Jimmy Brink, Carl Earn, and scores of the present juniors. If you leave an opening as you advance, do it because you're trying to get your opponent to hit for it so you can pounce on it, not because you have simply overlooked it or because you are rushing so you can't cover it. On the other hand, don't loaf in so lazily that you are caught at your feet by your opponent's shot, and forced to half-volley the ball.

The volley as I have described it and its use so far is the solid, fast, deep, blocked volley which is used the vast majority of times. However, there is another volley, the soft, drop volley with backspin, which is very valuable, though secondary to the blocked shot. It plays the same role to the block volley that the slice does to the drive—as variation, and to surprise and disconcert your opponent. This volley is hit in the same way as the block, except that the wrist is loosened slightly, and a little chop is imparted to backspin the ball. It is almost like a "tap" against the ball. The racquet head passes down and under the ball, and the bounce is low, and has "drag." The shot, to be effective, must never go more than ten feet into your opponent's court, and preferably at an angle. The shorter the shot and the sharper the angle, the better. This volley, like the slice, is most effective on clay and grass, has very little value on hard courts like concrete, and has almost none on wood. Any surface that causes the ball to bound high and forward practically nullifies its use. The delicate "touch" variety of volley is definitely secondary in importance to the volley that carries pace and depth from a flat, solid racquet, but both are needed in the equipment of a real tennis player.

The second shot in the net game is

THE OVERHEAD SMASH

This is the big gun of tennis. Here, more than anywhere else, brute force and sheer power pay off. I do not mean that there is no place for brains, for there is in mixing in the slow angle, but most overheads are won by the speed of the shot alone.

*Eye fixed on
approaching ball—body
sideways—racquet prepared*

*Leaning into the shot—
racquet head traveling ahead
of hand at moment of impact*

The technique of the smash is simple. Model it on the cannonball service.

1. Keep your eye on the ball until you hit it. More overheads are missed because a player looks down just before he hits the ball and, by so doing, pulls his racquet head off the line of his shot, than for any other cause.

2. Turn sideways and, even if the ball is a little to the left of your head, hit it as a forehand. There is no such shot as a backhand overhead.

3. Keep at least one foot on the ground and do not rotate your body to face the court until you have hit the ball, but lean into your shot as you hit.

4. Take a full arm swing and be sure that the racquet head is traveling ahead of your hand at the moment the ball is hit.

5. Hit absolutely flat, directly at the point you want the ball to go, and continue your swing to the very end of the racquet head arc, down to below your knees.

Flat follow-through toward point at which shot is directed

The swing is modeled on the Cannonball service

The overhead is always an attacking shot in theory, and it should be hit with great decision. Only if a ball is so high and deep that you must jump to reach it should it be played defensively. Many players, such as Borotra, Cochet, Gonzales, Bob Falkenberg, and Kramer, go all out for their kill, even when leaping off the ground with both feet. No matter how far back you may be driven by a lob, you must always lean forward into your smash as you make it. Once more I must stress that it is the racquet head and the speed of its swing that give the power and pace to the stroke. Great overheads are made with little or no body movement, no convulsive efforts, and an apparent ease that belies the power of the shot. The overhead is almost the only shot, except possibly the cannonball service, in which height is a great asset. However, it is not an absolute essential, as proved by Henri Cochet, a man of medium height but the possessor of one of the finest overheads in tennis history. It is the fluid swing of Cochet's racquet head that gives him his power.

Almost always, whenever the overhead can be used, it should be hit with destructive force. However, there are certain remarkable baseline players who can get to practically any shot hit deep, and put even the best fast overhead back into play. Frank Parker, Bobby Riggs, and Carl Earn are such players. When you're up against a "getter" of this sort, there comes a time to vary your tactics and bring in the slow, short, sharply angled overhead. If you have hit a couple of deep, fast overheads only to see them lobbed back high in the air, on the next one take the same preparation, but instead of swinging hard at the ball, bring the racquet against it on one side surface or the other of the ball. Make a sharp angle and block the ball as in a volley, off to the side instead of swinging through. This shot is valuable on clay or grass, since it will stay short, but on hard courts it is very dangerous to try. Under any circumstances, if you try it, follow your shot and close off the straight passing shot, for your opponent, if not caught napping by surprise, may reach it.

The whole story of the net game is *attack*. The net game has great strategic value if used intelligently at the right times, even though it is certainly not a game to play all the time, or thoughtlessly. If you have little else in your stroke equipment, you must fail a large percentage of the time. All your opponent needs is a sound enough defense to cope with your net game, and enough attack of his own to keep you away from the net part of the time.

Yet I consider the net game absolutely essential to every tennis player's equipment. All I hope is that he will not be carried away by its flashiness, and give it overemphasis. There is always an answer to anything, and I have attempted to show that in the ground stroke lies the answer to the net game.

CHAPTER 11

The Subtle Shots: The Lob;
The Half-Volley; The Drop Shot

THERE IS another ally of the ground stroke in its defense against the net rusher. It is one which, in the past decade, has been almost forgotten in singles, yet it is actually one of the most valuable and intelligent shots in singles as well as in doubles. (In doubles, its virtues have always been recognized.)

This shot is the lob, which is nothing more than a return of a stroke with a high toss of the ball in the air. There are three types of lob:

1. The slice or backspin lob (defense).
2. The flat lob (defense).
3. The loop or topspin lob (attack).

1. The Slice Lob. This is simply a chop stroke made with a definite tilting of the racquet back so that the flight of the ball, meeting the face of the racquet, is angled back up into the air. Control is gained by adding a little wrist flick, and there is very little backswing or follow-through.

2. The Flat Lob. To hit a flat lob, just drop the flat racquet face under the ball and hit it high in the air. It has not enough spin to control it, and is not as good as the slice lob.

3. The Loop or Topspin. This is a very daring, dangerous shot that is almost a trick shot. To hit it, drop your racquet head below the ball, hit up the back of the ball with a distinct lift, and turn your wrist over the ball, imparting a very heavy forward rotation. This will toss the ball about ten to twenty feet in the air and bring it down suddenly just behind the service line of your opponent's court. It is valuable only when your opponent is almost on top of the net and is expecting a drive. Frankly, I do not advise this shot; I believe that the slice lob, played at the unexpected time, will produce the same result with much less chance of error.

The slice lob is the most widely used lob and is purely a defensive measure, used when in difficulty to give you time to recover position. It is a slice or chop stroke, hit at a very high trajectory because the racquet head is tilted backward instead of being flat. There is very little in the way of variety to this shot. It is hit with the Continental or Eastern service grip (number 3) and is played the same way off forehand and backhand. The easiest way to describe the shot is to say you just bump the ball up in the air without much swing but giving it a definitely sliced or backspin quality. The reason for the backspin is that the spin, working against the air, holds and retards the flight of the ball, controls the distance of its flight, and gives you more time to recover position before your opponent hits his next shot. This shot should always be played high, at least twenty feet or more in the air, and as deep as you dare into your opponent's court. Remember you are not trying to win the point with this shot but to keep the ball in play while you get back into position, and perhaps get an error from your opponent. Therefore, allow yourself a good margin of safety. Your chief danger is that you will lob too short and give your opponent an easy kill. Therefore, risk your lob going over the baseline rather than hitting too short or too low. Make good use of the greatest distance you can—so send most lobs on the diagonal, or cross-court. As a general rule, the lob going toward your opponent's backhand corner is very valuable, but it also may allow him to try the angle smash into your backhand, if your lob is not high and deep enough to put him on the defensive. The lob to the forehand corner is good if it is played unexpectedly. It may catch your opponent off balance. Do not lob every time you get into difficulties. So many players make this mistake. The moment they are pushed by an attacking shot sending them wide, they "poop" the ball up. All the opponent needs to do is come halfway in and wait for it. Most singles players of today seem to fall into either of two classes: the ones who never lob, and the ones who always lob when attacked. The lob is of value only when it is played as part of the pattern of the whole game, and not simply a shot set apart. It should be used at the unexpected moments, not when it seems certain to be played.

In these days of modern net rushers who don't seem to understand that there is such a shot as the lob, a clever player will occasionally mix in a slice lob in place of the usual short, soft drive. This often works well because, in the first place, the net rusher is moving forward so fast that the lob may well go over his head for a winner, or catch him so off balance that he will miss his attempted overhead. Second, after a couple of lobs have been tossed over him, the net rusher begins to slow up on his advance, so that your chance to pass him with a fast drive is greatly increased, and at least your slow short shot now catches him at his feet as he comes in. Once again the effect of the lob pays off not only for itself, but also by increasing the value of your other shots.

Another use for the lob, which many players forget and which wins by its element of surprise, is off a short volley when your opponent closes in on top of the net to cut off your passing shot. Go low with your racquet and with a flat racquet face push the ball high and not too deep. You must get it up high enough to get over the fully extended racquet reach of the net player. He cannot go back after it, since he is already moving forward to make a killing volley off your expected drive. Closely allied to this shot is the lob-volley in doubles. It can be used only when all four players are close in at the net, and it, too, is just a high toss over either man. Both the lob off the short bound and the lob-volley win entirely by their surprise element, and unless you play them with no indication of your intention, you will get them rammed down your throat by the return kill from the net player.

The ways to use the lob are:

1. When it is unexpected and not the shot that your opponent would look for, particularly when he is advancing to the net and is prepared for a passing drive.
2. When you are drawn in directly in front of your opponent at the net and he jumps in on top of the net.
3. When you are forced so far out of court that you require a lot of time to regain position.

The lob, in singles, is a prime example of one of the refinements of the game that has been overlooked in the past decade. It is one of the most valuable, and it is time to bring it back into its proper place in tennis strategy.

We come now to the trimmings, the shots that are the last word in the game and the strokes that need not be taught. When a player reaches the place where he should use them, he is good enough to evolve his own way to play them, because they are largely a matter of "feel," or tennis instinct. These shots are:

1. The half-volley or pickup.
2. The drop shot.

I will not coach these shots, except where an already completely equipped player requests it, because I believe no player should monkey with either one until he is master of all the other strokes. However, I am going to give an idea of the shots and discuss their uses.

1. **The Half-Volley or Pickup.** Its very name is confusing, and really a misnomer. It is actually a drive, not a volley at all. It is a rising bounce drive played just as the ball starts to rise from the ground, and should be hit with the grip, footwork, backswing, and complete stroke production of the drive—forehand or backhand. Except, of course, the ball can't be taken waist-high. The real secret in hitting a half-volley lies in bending the knees, so you crouch over the ball, leaning into the shot and following through to the end of your swing with a flat racquet face and a stiff wrist. The common error most players commit is standing up straight and shoveling or blocking the ball, instead of following through and making it a real

stroke. The half-volley should be played only when you are forced to do so, because you've been caught with a shot at your feet. It should not be deliberately chosen. Your better choice, if you are in the back court, is to move back and let the ball rise to your waist before you play it. If you are in mid-court or closer to the net, move in and play a low volley.

Since the half-volley is more or less a desperation shot made under pressure, play it for attack, not defense. Hit it firmly, decisively, and fairly hard, moving in with your shot as you make it. If you fall away from the ball, or attempt to half-volley it while moving backward, you will balloon your shot far out or up. If you always regard the shot as a rising bounce drive, played at the earliest possible moment, you can at times use a half-volley as an advancing shot to go to the net behind, but it should only be done if your opponent is far out of court and you are attempting to hurry him to the limit. It is dangerous but, if successful, very effective. There is no shot in tennis that requires the perfect split-second timing that the half-volley does. Above all, it demands perfect vision, with the eye never leaving the ball for even an instant. It is fun to play, but its likely percentage of error is so high that it should be used only when there is no other possible shot.

2. **The Drop Shot.** This is nothing more than a very delicate slice or chop shot, made with the racquet head tilted backward about halfway between the slice and the lob techniques. It requires quite a little wrist flick, very little backswing, and a fair follow-through. The racquet head must meet the ball fairly solidly, but pass under it imparting distinct backspin. The shot definitely rises in the air and should have a safe clearance of a few feet above the net line at the top of its arc. It must fall within eight feet or less of the net to be of any real value. If your shot goes too deep, it is just a setup. Be careful when you play it, and above all do not play it too much. Its greatest chance of success lies in its element of surprise, which obviously, will be lost if it is overused.

The drop shot is most effective after you have run a man

into a deep corner. Then drop the ball cross-court, within about eight feet of the net and close to the far sideline.

The effects of the drop, like those of the slice, are cumulative. It is comparatively easy to reach in the first set, but after you have chased drops often enough for four sets, they begin to look a long way off.

Both the half-volley and the drop shot vary greatly in effectiveness with the court surface, and in exactly opposite ways. The half-volley is a comparatively easy shot and very effective on wood and hard courts, like concrete. The trueness of the court surface and the fact that spin takes little hold make it easy to time your shot, but on grass and clay, which are slower and not so true, the half-volley becomes extremely hard to time and dangerous to play. On the other hand, the drop shot, with its backspin and soft pace, is deadly on clay and grass, but on hard courts and wood, where the spin doesn't hold and the bound is higher, it is useless unless absolutely perfectly disguised.

So ends the section of this book dealing with the strokes of tennis. I have pointed out their techniques and main uses. Let me once more sound a warning against thinking that strokes themselves mean everything, or make a good tennis player. You may hit a ball with perfect form, look like a million dollars on the court, and be a complete pushover for an opponent. I have tried to stress the need to think on every shot. Never hit a ball without a definite idea of how it will affect you—and your opponent. While it is essential to know *how* to hit a tennis ball, in every stroke it is the *why, where,* and *when* of it that wins tennis matches.

Now that you have an idea of the strokes and how they can be used, you are ready to take up the most important things in tennis—the tactics and psychology of the game. How are matches won, and what is it that turns a loser into a winner? The next section of this book deals with those factors, which change a person from somebody who plays tennis into a Tennis Player, and perhaps into a Champion.

PART THREE

MATCH PLAY TACTICS AND TENNIS PSYCHOLOGY

CHAPTER 12

Courage

OVER THE ENTRANCE to the great center court at Wimbledon, England, and also over the marquee steps to the stadium at the West Side Tennis Club, Long Island, are identical signs. They carry two lines from Rudyard Kipling's "If":

If you can meet with Triumph and Disaster
And treat those two impostors just the same. . . .

In those two lines, Kipling gave the perfect picture of what a great tennis player must have, and both tennis associations, British and American, recognized it. It is a long but effective way of saying one word—Courage! When I use the term "courage" here, I do not merely mean that wonderful quality that is part of courage, known colloquially as "guts." Certainly that quality is also needed by a champion, but it is momentary, perhaps fleeting, and but an infinitesimal part of the entire picture of courage.

Courage embodies patience, philosophy, and the vision to lift your eyes to the goal far ahead. It is the ability, in spite of discouragement, disheartening disappointments, even apparent failure, never to lose sight of that goal, or belief in yourself and your ultimate victory.

It takes five years to make a Tennis Player and ten years to make a Champion. If you set out to be champion, you must have the courage to look ten years ahead, and never waver or hesitate, even during those awful periods of growing pains when your game seems to be getting nowhere. You will lose to players you know you should beat, and all your best friends either look the other way when you play or tell you bluntly that you are just a dub and always will be. Every great player goes through such periods. I know I did. I wish I had a dollar for every time I definitely made up my mind at night that I'd give up the game forever. Many were the evenings when I burned my racquets in imagination, only to be out on the court the next day, just as full of enthusiasm, confidence, and love of the game as ever. Perhaps that quality isn't courage, only pigheadedness, but whatever it is, a person must have it, if he is ever going to become a real Tennis Player.

Progress in tennis is usually slow and not very easy to see. There are long periods in the development of every first-class player when he feels he is standing still. Do not look for improvement on a day-to-day or week-to-week basis. If you're lucky and going up fast, the quickest visible improvement is month by month, but it is more likely to be a seasonal one. It takes patience and philosophy to get you over this hump. The sounder and more carefully you lay your foundation, the better grounded in technique your strokes during your early years, the slower may be the progress. You may get some terrible lickings from flashy naturals who have played only half as long as you have, and whose strokes look like windmills. You may find yourself wondering why you waste all this time on correct form when, in a short time, some dub with no idea what he's doing can beat you. "Perhaps," you tell yourself, "I'm crazy and I'd better give it all up." That is the time your courage must come to your aid and keep your eyes on that distant goal of perfection. It can keep you plugging, and if it does, about a year later, you run into the same dub and you make a remarkable discovery—now he's a pushover. You beat him so easily, you wonder how you could ever have lost to him. Actually, during that year, all you did was to gain mastery of what you had, but had not been able to control, a year before.

Every stroke that you gain control of, so that it is really dependable, takes at least six months of hard, intensive work in actual match play. If you make the mistake of attempting to work on too many shots at a time, you will gain control of none. The service and ground strokes can be learned and worked on together, but for your first year you should not attempt anything about the net game beyond learning the mere mechanics. The next year you can afford to start going in a great deal. In fact, turn for a while from a baseliner to a net player, and then gradually blend the two styles. The third year you can start to mix in the backspin shots, and soft volley. The fourth, you should take to work on variation of strokes and variety of spin, speed, and pace. Finally, you add the half-volley and drop shot, and if you have reasonable control of all these, you have become a Tennis Player, instead of just someone who plays tennis. You can see that patience, determination, and vision of the ultimate goal are required to carry you along this sort of road. An added difficulty is the fact that each new shot you start to learn upsets to some extent the ones you have already mastered, with the result that each year you will suffer some unexpected and discouraging defeats. Once the technical mastery of all these shots is yours, then experimentation in match play is needed to show when and where each will serve you best. It will take you several years to gain the knowledge that you will need to meet all players and all situations. During that time you will still lose matches to players you know you should beat, but you will have the inspiration of a few upset victories over stars who are as surprised as you are at the result. Those victories are merely the signposts of your regular game of the future, and you should treasure them to boost your courage for the long road to tennis heights. Do not make the mistake of considering that one or two good wins means your job is done. They are merely indications of what is to come in the next few years. Many young players get delusions of grandeur after their first few big victories. They suddenly realize that they are God's gift to tennis, that they know all there is to know about the game, and right there they start down the path to tennis oblivion. Confidence and belief in one's self are almost essential to success, but conceit is the one certain poison to kill all chance of it. Take your victories and defeats in your stride, and keep your feet on the ground and your head a trifle smaller than your hat. Success is a dangerous wine, particularly to the young. It can make you as drunk with your own importance as any liquor. It is during the time of your first successes that the philosophical quality of your courage must come to your aid. All those good old bromides like "The bigger they come, the harder they fall" carry real truth. Take your game seriously and regard it with respect. Play it always to the best of your ability, but for heaven's sake don't believe your publicity and start taking yourself too seriously. Conceit and fatheadedness can ruin your physical condition, your match temperament, and your future in an incredibly short time.

One of the early symptoms of conceit is an attitude of disparagement toward one's opponent and his game. This is a growing attitude today among the juniors, and a most distressing one. I have watched so many kids recently who seemed to take a good shot by their opponent as a personal insult instead of giving it the admiration that was its due. Instead of saying "Good shot!" sincerely, as a true sportsman would, they say "Good God!," meaning "How dare he hit such a shot at me? Doesn't he know who I am?" I see these same juniors barely get a racquet on a passing shot by making a great effort, for which they deserve credit, and then cry in anguish, "How can I miss an easy shot like that?," when actually it would have beaten any player in the world. All these things are outward manifestations of an ingrowing conceit that will ruin these kids, unless caught and restrained by themselves. Unfortunately, these offenders hate to admit any other person's equality, let alone superiority. The present crop of alibis for defeat is the greatest of any period in tennis history. Perhaps this is due to the tremendous amount of publicity that results whenever there is an upset, or a remarkable match is played. If so, the attitude is wrong, for it is based on fear. Franklin Roosevelt put his finger on that fatal disease when he said, "All we have to fear is fear itself." Behind much of conceit is fear, rooted in an inferiority complex and camouflaged by the swagger and the boast. There are many dangerous, regrettable examples of such conceit in the tennis world. One finds the player who, having won a good match, avoids his defeated opponent thereafter whenever possible, afraid to give him another chance, but he always lets the world know he won the last time they met. There is the reverse situation where the player, once beaten, tries to stay away from any event where he might meet his conqueror again, afraid of another licking. There is the great practice player, the man who hits like a

demon when he is playing for fun, but who, when the chips are down
in a match, ladles everything and loses ignominiously. Yet he always
tells of his great victories in practice, and invariably forgets his tournament record. All these players are on the wrong foot. They are afraid!
Play tennis without fear of defeat and because it's fun and you enjoy
it, or don't play it at all. There is no disgrace in defeat. The only disgrace lies in quitting in or "dogging" a match. There is no disgrace, no
blot on your escutcheon, in admitting that there are players who can
beat you, either in a match, a set, or on any given shot. You don't have
to try to prove it was an accident. In the first place, nobody believes
you, so you simply appear ridiculous, and in the second place, nobody
cares but you, and you know the truth. All these alibis and explana-
tions take your mind off the really important thing, which is, or should
be, your match. If done to excess this sort of thing will destroy your
concentration and bring about the very thing you fear, defeat.

There is no time in any hard-fought tennis match for your mind to
wander if you want to win. Conceit makes you too self-conscious and
is apt to set your mind thinking about how you look, or what the gallery is saying about you, when it should be centered on your tactics
and your opponent. There is a great difference between confidence
and conceit, but many players never find out what it is. The knowledge of what you have in your own game, the sincere belief that it will
win, *provided* it is played to the best of your ability and the limit of
your physical resources if necessary—that is confidence, and it will
carry you far. The attitude that you are so good you need not try, that
you are so great that your opponent must fear you, and that you are
past the point where you can learn anything more is conceit. That will
beat you consistently and if it becomes a habit will completely ruin
your game. The dividing line is very thin, and extremely easy to cross.
You should be on your guard at all times against the insidious inroads
of your ego. Once more, you must call on the vision of the distant
goal to keep your balance. Believe me, you are never as good as they
tell you you are, when you're winning, and never as bad as you think
you are in defeat. A player plays as well as his opponent allows him
to play. If you recognize the fact that many of your errors are due

to the cleverness of your opponent and not just to your being "off your game," you will be able to stay in your match and fight much better than if you're stewing in your own juice because you are attempting to explain your errors to the world. Conceit makes you far too conscious of your own mistakes and makes you dwell on them. Confidence allows you to take them in stride, forget them, and play the next point. There is a turning point in every player's career where he reaches the peak of progress and, after a period at the top, he starts downhill. The beginning of that turn is very hard to detect. The period at the peak of one's game may be long or short, but once that strange little turn comes, the decline is apt to be steady. The turn is completely psychological, and quite apart from a physical decline due to a definite accident, injury, illness, or age. The exact moment a player passes his peak is when he no longer plays to win, but only not to lose. In other words, it takes place when the possibility or probability of defeat is always in his mind, and he plays only to ward it off. Once more the specter of fear is haunting him. Many young players take years trying to overcome this, and their progress is retarded. If they do not rise above it, they never become real Players. There are even more youngsters who have so strong a natural belief in their ability to win that they never know what it is to expect defeat, and are surprised each time they are defeated, as they so often are, in their early stages. Still, that optimism is absolutely necessary to progress, since, if you are to go forward, you must always play to win, expect victory, and fight for it to the end. If it doesn't come, surprise is natural and healthy.

Before you can really "dish it out" in tennis, you have to learn to "take it." Only by going through the mill of many defeats can a player gain the experience needed to show him what shot to play, and when and where to play it. Champions are born in the labor of defeat. It takes all phases of courage to go through the years when defeat is your portion a large part of the time, and realize, amid all your discouragement, that you are steadily forging ahead toward your goal. If you learn something of tactics or the psychology of match play in a losing match, as you should if you analyze it afterward, you have taken another step toward the complete mastery of your game.

CHAPTER 13

Exploiting Your
Opponent's Weaknesses

TENNIS matches are won by the man who hits the ball to the right place at the right time most often. That right place may be determined by the possibility of making a clean winner, but more often it's a place from which an opponent will make an error on his return shot. Nothing is so disconcerting or upsetting to a player as to miss. A magnificent shot, which beats him completely, doesn't cause him much mental anguish because, if he is a sportsman, he will admire it and then not worry about it any more. On the other hand, each time he sees an important shot of his own sail out of court or into the net, a player becomes more nervous and less likely to win a match. The more errors he makes, the less likely are his chances of pulling his game together on subsequent points. Remember that in first-class tournament tennis, 70 per cent of all points end in error, a net or an out, and only 30 per cent end in winning placements or service aces. (Of course, the percentage of points ending in an error is even higher in poorer-caliber tennis.)

This fact gives birth to the first great rule in general tactics:

Keep the ball in play and give your opponent another shot at it, rather than risk an error by taking an unnecessary chance.

Notice the word "unnecessary" in that rule. Naturally, if you are presented with a weak shot, be ready to take advantage of it. But the keynote of good tactics is to be content to keep the ball going and move your opponent around his court unless:

1. You see the big opening and decide to hit out for a winner, or
2. You are forced into an almost hopeless position, with little chance to extricate yourself, and you decide that the gamble carries practically no extra risk, and may conceivably turn the tables in your favor.

Let your opponent be the one to take the *unnecessary* chances, and the one who will pile up the majority of those 70 per cent errors. You are playing the percentage if you do so, and you'll beat your opponent if you are otherwise evenly matched. However, always be ready for the opening to win outright, while you are keeping the ball going. You are "playing your hooked fish"—getting ready to land him. The best tennis tacticians play *a defensive game with an offensive mental attitude.*

The first thought that you should have, when you step onto a court for a match, is "What are my opponent's weaknesses? Where will he miss most?" You should start at once, even during the warm-up, to watch for the signs that point to weaknesses.

The beginning of any tennis match has somewhat the same quality as that shown by two boxers, feeling each other out before risking their respective attacks. Much of that exploration can be achieved during the warm-up period if you are clever about it, and the chances are that your opponent will be quite unaware of the fact that you are doing anything except warming up. The way to do it is to vary your first shots to him: a drive, a chop—a fast shot, then a slow one. Stick in a mid-court shot and watch what he does with it. Does he walk in and hit it hard, and then come in to volley, or does he just hit it back, and then retire to the baseline again? Did he show any sign of hesitancy in hitting your backspin slice? Did he attempt to meet speed with speed, or did he show timidity in returning your fast drives? What was the form of his ground strokes?

You should be able to get some leading hints about two aspects of your opponent's tennis game by the end of the warm-up period. They are:

1. The type of game he will probably elect to play against you, which, unless he knows something about you, is undoubtedly his most natural and strongest game.
2. Any weaknesses in stroke production he may have, which are likely to be obvious if the form of his ground strokes is faulty in certain respects.

Let's take up these two aspects in detail, and see what indications your opponent may give you that will help you determine how to plan your own offense.

1. The Type of Game Your Opponent Will Probably Play. If, at the end of the warm-up, you are of the opinion that he is going to defend from the baseline and doesn't like speed, you should attack in the first game, going to the net behind fast drives. If, on the other hand, you think he will turn out to be a slugger (a much more likely thing these days), start your match in a slow, soft tempo, using distinct variation of spin and depth. By so doing you are attempting to upset the hitter at the very outset, by forcing errors from him. In any case, start all matches with a slow enough tempo and pace so that your own energies will be able to build in power and pressure, no matter how long the match continues. The modern "neck or nothing" type of game usually goes off like an explosion, but if the original impetus fails to carry to victory, there is no reserve left for a rally. You should space every match so that you still have a final physical and mental reserve to call upon, a little unexpended energy to bring up for victory in a final set. Too many players waste valuable energy in rushing a match unnecessarily. The wise player learns to relax *physically* between points, games, and sets, even though he can never relax *mentally* until the match is over.

Walk, don't run, into position. Don't stall deliberately, but you are entitled to a reasonable time in which to get ready, so take it, even if your opponent is stewing and fidgeting to get started on a point. Play your own game, not his. If you are playing a rusher, slow up the tempo. If you are up against a staller, keep him moving a shade faster than he likes. There is nothing unsporting about this—

you are simply taking your rights under the rules. The proper tempo of a match for you is the one you like, and you should make every effort to set it. When two players start a match, it is always a battle to see who will dominate the match, and who will be pushed around. One player or the other will ultimately impress his tennis personality on the other. The one who does will win, because by so doing he forces the recognition of impending defeat upon his opponent. One of the surest ways to achieve this state of affairs is to set your own tempo and hold it. Do it courteously, with all due regard to your opponent's rights, but do it. An attitude of calm confidence goes a long way toward maintaining a mental edge. The more you can make your opponent feel that you expect to win, intend to win, and there's nothing he can do to shake your confidence and determination, the harder it is for him to hold his own concentration. That old school bromide, "A man who won't be beaten can't be beaten," may be ripe corn, but there's a lot of truth in it.

2. **Weaknesses in Stroke Production Your Opponent May Display by the Form of His Ground Strokes.** During the warm-up period, there are several definite indications of this sort which you can use later to your advantage.

   a. *The form of the shot, particularly with respect to the backswing and feet.* If you meet a player with a roundhouse backswing, starting high, or a man who faces the net while making a stroke, you will know at once that he is vulnerable to a low, backspin shot into the deep corners. He is also an easy mark for a speedy shot aimed directly at him, since he will be caught with his racquet too high and forced to crowd his return. Any player who faces the net when he hits his shots can't get down to the ball and still keep his body out of the way of his swing, on low, short shots. He will also have trouble on shots that keep going away from him and make him reach, since he cannot throw his weight out on a balancing foot, as he could if he stroked from the sideways position. Therefore, the sharply angled cross-court shot will tie this man into knots.

b. *A definite tendency to run around a ball that should be played on the backhand, and to take it on the forehand.* The fact that your opponent is so eager to stay away from playing a shot off his backhand means that he is weak off that side, but watch out in trying to exploit that weakness. He has probably built up his greatest strength, his forehand drive made from his backhand court, to cover it. J. O. Anderson, the Australian Davis Cup star of a quarter of a century ago, was such a player, and only really dangerous when he could pound his pet forehand from the backhand court. The way to play this obvious weakness is to hit once to the side or corner of the forehand court, in order to open up the backhand court, and then attack the latter. Against a man with a backhand weakness, it is also good to go to the net once you have placed the ball solidly on that side, for the return is likely to be a weak one.

c. *A tendency to hang back on the baseline when it is logical to come to net.* This probably means your opponent possesses an uncertain volley or overhead. Try him out early in the match by using short shots, and even a drop shot or two. Then, if he stays in at the net, as he almost must do, hit directly at him once with great speed, try one soft, angled passing shot, and toss up a lob. His method of playing these shots will confirm your suspicions if he is poor at certain aspects of net play. If he is, draw him in whenever possible, and then give him every chance to make errors by playing to his weakness.

d. *A continuous net attack.* This is likely to mean uncertain ground strokes. You should use every method, including lobbing, to force your opponent away from the net during the early games. If unsuccessful in doing so, go in a good deal on your own service, so that at least he is forced to play every second game from the back court. That will offer enough of a chance for his weakness to show up, if he has it.

All of the above can be summed up in another important tactical rule: *Never give your opponent a shot he likes to play if you can avoid it.* (There is an exception to this rule, which will be discussed a little later on, but the rule is an excellent one under most circumstances.)

No one, not even the greatest tactician in the world, can lay down specific rules of tactics for any given point, or series of points, and have them work every time. You may start a point with a definite idea of just how you will play it to win, have things seem to be going well, and then any one of several occurrences may take place and force you to change your plans. You may play a weaker or shorter shot than you intended, and your opponent will take the attack away from you. Or you may start out to exploit your opponent's weakness only to have him make a lucky shot off it, or even an unexpectedly good shot, which leaves him in a favorable position if you continue the attack you planned. Or you may have guessed wrong on what your opponent himself planned to do. He may come in when you thought he was going to stay back, with the result that carrying through your original plan would now be fatal. In all of these circumstances, and others like them, you must discard your original ideas and bring up fresh ones to meet the new situation.

Do not be mechanical or pigheaded about your tactics. Always keep an open mind, aware of the whole picture and ready to change plans at any time if it seems wise. Far too many players make up their minds to play a certain point, game, set, or even match in one way, and stick to it even when it's obvious that they're getting nowhere with it. That is neither courage nor determination—it is stupidity. There are two generalities of tactics which should be borne in mind in this connection:

Never change a winning game.

Always change a losing game.

The first seems obvious. You would think that anyone would know enough to follow that rule, but for some perverse reason it seems to work the other way with some players. A man will build up a winning lead by staying back and pounding his opponent's backhand. Then suddenly, for no understandable reason except perhaps a desire to finish in a blaze of glory, he begins to rush the net, starts losing points, and ends by being defeated. Perhaps the reverse takes place. He builds up his lead by going to the net constantly but, just as he should be finishing his man off, suddenly retires to the baseline and eventually loses. Perhaps he gains his lead by slow finesse and changes to speed for no reason, or vice versa. In each case he changes a winning game before he has won, and by doing so he gets just what he deserves —a licking.

Conversely, it is equally stupid to insist upon playing to the end a type of game that is losing badly. If you do, you are certain to lose. You may lose anyway, but you might better try to win with something else. If you can't win from the baseline, go to the net. If you have been going in, and it hasn't been working, stay back and see if you can out-steady your opponent. Try out something new, if what you have previously been trying has failed.

There is another approach to this tactical problem, which is that your opponent is never completely beaten until you have broken his morale, and made him conscious of his impending defeat. Pounding a weakness is one way to do it. It is the longest, often the surest, and certainly the most universally used method. A method I frequently prefer is quicker, more exciting, and perhaps more dangerous, but if it's successful it inflicts the most lasting of all defeats. It is *to play your opponent's strength until you break it.* (This, of course, is the exception to the tactical rule of not giving your opponent a shot he likes to play.) Believe me, once a player finds his favorite shot won't win for him, his whole game collapses. If he can't win with his strength, he can't win at all. Once a player admits defeat to himself he is through, even though he plays on gamely, and tries to hide it. Certainly, the very fact that you attack his strong point with assurance and confidence will shake him, if you get away with it a few times. It makes him aware of your strength of purpose and will to win, and keeps tremendous mental pressure on him that is worth much to you in a long match. It takes courage and determination on your part to attack his strength, but if you do it of your own volition you are prepared for his reply, and you can tune your own game accordingly.

Finally, in sizing up your opponent, be prepared for the deliberate "goat-getter," the man who consciously sets out to irritate you and destroy your concentration. If you are prepared for him you have the battle half won before it starts. The goat-getter is usually a fresh gent who starts out by telling you, or hinting to you on the way to the court, how easily he will win. He then is apt to stall around and generally foul up the court so that it's almost impossible to set a tempo to the match and hold it. He isn't really trying to set a tempo to the pace of the play, which is what I have advised you to do; he is merely attempting to upset you by his disregard of ordinary tennis court manners. The greatest weapon against the goat-getter is to ignore his verbal or physical "needling" completely. Go your own way, pay no attention to his remarks, play if anything a shade more slowly than he does, and give no show of irritation even if you are burning up inside.

But do not go out onto the court looking for trouble. Most players are good sportsmen, and their occasional lapses from courtesy are due to thoughtlessness or carelessness, and are not intentional. You can always delude yourself into believing you are being cheated or needled, if you start looking for trouble. If you do, you can completely destroy your own concentration, even though the fancied offense that bothered may not really have been present at all. Close calls can always give rise to differences of opinion, but just call them as you see them, without prejudice or favor. Call them as impersonally in your own match as you would if you were a linesman in a match between strangers. Only on the shot on which you are really uncertain should you give the benefit of the doubt to your opponent. If you are fair and impartial yourself and believe your opponent to be the same, you are playing the game. You may both make mistakes at times, but they will be honest mistakes and they should be forgotten, with no hard feelings, by the next point. Thinking about past points you have lost, whether because of bad decisions or unlucky breaks, only costs you present points as well, because your mind is not on your job.

CHAPTER 14

General Tactics and Strategy

THE FIRST-CLASS court general and tactician is the man who not only knows all the technical answers but is also trying to exploit the psychological element to the detriment of his opponent. Such a man is always consciously aware of the logical reply to the shot his opponent plays, and also which sequence of shots of his own will pay off most frequently. He knows that he must wait out all spin shots until they have crossed the top of the bound. A slice or chop (or even, to a lesser degree, a heavily topped drive) carries all the "devil" with which it has been hit through the air, right on through its bounce to the top of the bound. Until that point, it is almost certain to twist off the racquet face and slide away as an error unless your return stroke is perfectly timed. However, at the top of the bound the spin dies, and as the ball falls it can be hit as easily and surely as if it were the bounce off a flat shot. If you do try to take a spin shot before it reaches the top of the bound, hit it flat and firmly to kill the effect of the spin. Do not chop a chop.

Here are some axioms on the best ways of handling your returns of various strokes:

1. The answer to a chop is a drive.
2. The answer to a drive may be either a drive or a chop—a drive for attack, and a chop for defense.
3. The answer to a smash is usually a lob, occasionally a drive or a chop.
4. The answer to a volley is usually a drive, occasionally a lob.
5. The answer to speed is backspin.
6. The answer to backspin is the flat drive.

There are certain mechanical combinations of shots that are sound tactically, provided you do not become so wedded to them that you play them stubbornly every time, with no variations:

1. Three drives in a row to the same corner, and then a sharp, slow cross-court to the other side.
2. Four drives from alternate corner to corner, and then the cross-court drop shot.
3. Alternate corner to corner until you decide your opponent is set in the rhythm, and then the slow, straight short shot back to the same side of court as your last shot.
4. First a drop shot, then a lob deep to the opposite side of the court.
5. First a drive, then a chop, then a drive, then a chop, and so forth, with continually varying depth until an error is forced.

These are only a few samples of the sorts of pattern an acute court strategist knows; he's always ready to try out new and unexpected things also. He watches his opponent make his shot, so he can be prepared to handle whatever spin may be hit at him. Watching the place an opponent's racquet head meets the ball will always give you the tip-off on the direction in which the ball will bounce. If the ball is hit *above the waist*, it will bounce in the same direction as the racquet head was traveling when it hit and followed through on the ball. On the other hand, if an opponent hits the ball *below the waist*, the ball will bounce in the *opposite* direction from that in which the racquet head travels on the follow-through.

You should never hit any shot in match play without a definite intention behind it. If you drive, think of driving and of no other type of stroke. Even more important, on that shot think with decision where you will hit the ball, and why. Every shot should be hit to a definite place, in a definite way, for a definite purpose, and not just hit back over the net for no particular reason except to get it into your opponent's court. Make up your mind before you hit the ball that you are going to do one of three things:

1. Attack with this stroke, going out for an aggressive shot, or
2. Maneuver your opponent and open his court by playing a medium-pace shot, with a safe margin of error, to the widest reach away from his position, or

3. Defend with this stroke, if you sense you are in difficulty, by playing a slow floating drive or a well-spun slice, to change the tempo and give you time to recover.

Obviously, there are shots other than the ones cited above that you will sometimes use in these situations, but the point is that you must recognize that you are either going to attack, maneuver, or defend, and play your shot accordingly without vacillating.

Whichever of these three choices you decide upon, keep in mind the follow-up shot you will use if your opponent returns the ball. Are you going in to the net to win, or will you stay back and work on your opponent's position further before hitting out for the point? Where will his logical return come, and to what position should you move to be ready to meet it? And when it does come, what type of shot will your next one be?

Unless he is trying for an outright winner, a good player always hits his shot with his next shot in mind, and a really fine court general is usually planning two strokes in advance of the one he is then hitting. As particularized in detail earlier in this chapter, there are several. types of baseline rallies that, unless deliberately broken up by one player or the other, will follow an almost invariable pattern. The most general type is the cross-court exchange to deep court. The one seen most often is the backhand-to-backhand variety. The forehand-to-forehand variety seldom continues for more than three exchanges. To break up either type of cross-court exchange, there are two excellent shots. One is the faster straight shot, paralleling the sideline, into the deep corner. The other is a slow and very sharply angled cross-court shot, which is still in pattern with the exchange, but has very different depth and pace, and possibly has different spin as well.

Another rhythmic pattern you often see is one player hitting cross-court every time, and the other hitting straight returns. This makes both men run back and forth across the back court almost equal distances. To break this up, the man who has been hitting cross-court can insert a slow, high slice down the center, or straight. The man who has been hitting straight can break up the pattern by hitting a slow, sharply angled drive cross-court. Either of these methods changes the rhythm of the point and is very likely to force an error from the other man. Obviously, one way to break up any back-court exchange is for either player suddenly to go in to net. However, if the baseline exchanges are carrying good depth, it is a dangerous experiment and usually results in the advancing player being passed, or forced into error, while trying to get up far enough to reach a volley position. It is better to break up the rhythm of these back-court rallies by a change of pace, spin, depth, and direction from the baseline, than it is to risk an ill-considered and improperly prepared advance to the net.

One certain tactical stratagem is to decide what feature of your opponent's game you will attempt to exploit, and then hop on it at the beginning and never leave it until you are convinced it will not break. It may be his weakness or his strength, but whichever you elect, stay with it until you can see how the picture is working out. If you're winning with it, keep going the same way as long as the general tide of play is going in your favor. Only when you're convinced that the method you have selected isn't going to win for you should you change to something else, but be sure to do so then. Otherwise, stay with your plan of campaign the whole way. On individual points you often will be forced to change plans, and you must always use enough variety to keep your opponent guessing, but maintain one definite point upon which to center the pressure you are trying to apply, and do not wander from it. I often see players who seem just to be hitting a tennis ball with no very definite plan behind their play. For a while they hit to their opponent's forehand and then, for no reason, shift to his backhand. Or they stroll in toward net when they've made no proper preparation for an advance. If, behind these changes in play, there were real thought and reason for the shift, I would agree completely with the strategy, but when it's done without purpose it's sheer whim, and not strategy. It's valueless in that case. Consistent pressure centered on one point, disguised by enough variation to keep your purpose hidden, will produce the best results.

The margin of difference between a champion and a good tournament player is very small. Many times there is no difference in stroke equipment. I know many players with the finest technical games who have never made much of a mark in the tennis world. What is the dividing line between the champion and the merely good player? It lies in that intangible quality which makes the champion produce his best under pressure, and the other man his worst. I believe that the champion will miss just about as many shots as the second-class man, but he will miss them at different times. The champion seldom misses a shot he should make at a critical moment. His nerve never fails under pressure, whereas the second-class player, good as he is, misses in the pinch when playing the champion, and that's when it counts the most. It takes years of match play to school a player to make, and not err, when the match hangs on the result of a shot. He must be so completely master of himself and his game that he remains calm and confident, no matter how crucial the situation. I have always felt that Rudyard Kipling summed up the qualities of a champion as well as it can be done, in his lines from "If":

> *If you can force your heart and nerve and sinew*
> *To serve your turn long after they are gone,*
> *And so hold on when there is nothing in you*
> *Except the will which says to them: "Hold on."* . . .

Oh, yes! Those lines indeed describe a champion!

CHAPTER 15

Outside Conditions: Weather; Court Surface; The Entire Tournament Program

THERE ARE a number of extraneous factors, beyond the control of a player or his opponent, which can upset a star performer considerably, and can wreak havoc with the game of an ordinary player. A man who really understands how to take full advantage of unusual conditions has a big edge over one who doesn't. Nevertheless, it's the rare player who ever takes the trouble to study out what to do when up against such conditions as a strong wind or a bad court surface. Most players are so busy cursing the things that are bothering them, or crying in self-pity, that they forget to play tennis. One thing that few people realize is that bad conditions are great levelers of form. Most people think that bad conditions aid the better tennis player, if anything. Actually, the reverse is true, because the better player plays to a narrower margin of safety, normally. So it takes fewer and less severe unexpected difficulties to make him miss than it does the poorer player, who is not trying to do much more than merely hit the ball back over the net. However, the acute player who takes full cognizance of bad conditions, and then consciously plays to offset them or even to take advantage of them, can turn wind, slippery courts, or a torn-up court surface into assets rather than liabilities.

Wind. Because it is the most uncertain of the outside conditions, the wind is, perhaps, the most difficult one to offset. High wind invariably lowers the standard of play and presents the most difficult problems over and above the normal ones that exist under normal circumstances. I believe there are more upsets due to high wind than to any other single factor. There are no sure ways to offset a gale, but here are a few general things to remember when you're playing on a windy court.

1. Even greater concentration is required than at any other time.
2. Although it requires the earliest possible preparation of the racquet, you must hold your actual shot until the last moment.
3. It calls for a very short backswing, so the ball will not blow away while your racquet is coming forward on the stroke.
4. You must hit the ball solidly and decisively and use a long follow-through, or the ball will be blown all over the place.
5. Service should be hit with a rather reduced backswing, and hit flat.
6. Ground strokes: The drive should carry little spin, but should be hit flat and with plenty of power, so that the wind will have little chance to take hold of the ball. Always drive with the wind if possible; the spin on a slice or chop makes the ball soar too much. On the other hand, when playing against the wind, the chop is the more effective shot, although the drive may often be used.
7. The net game: When playing with the wind, go in whenever possible behind a drive, but do not try to use too much speed either on your advancing shot or on your volley or smash. All the advantage is with a net player in this situation, since an opponent's passing shot probably will be slowed down enough to enable the net player to reach it, and his lob may often be too short and allow the net player a kill. Conversely, don't try to go to net very often when playing against the wind yourself. If the wind is blowing cross-court, advance on the cross-court shot that goes with the wind and close off the straight-shot return.
8. Against a net player: Drive for a passing shot when the wind is with you. Lob very little with the wind, but use the lob a lot against the wind, and keep it deep. If you try a passing shot when playing into the wind, a slow, soft cross-court drive is your best selection.

If the wind is blowing cross-court, pass with a straight shot on the up-wind side, so the wind will tend to blow your shot into court.
9. Against the wind, the slice shot should be employed frequently, mixed in with the drive, and the drop shot should be tried fairly often as well.

Once more, let me emphasize that the constant keeping in mind of all of these points requires complete concentration on what you are doing at all times. When playing under windy conditions, force yourself to concentrate no matter what else you do.

The Slippery Court. The attacking game is handicapped tremendously on a slippery court because attack depends upon perfect footwork, which, on a slippery court, is almost impossible. Therefore, the net game can be used only sparingly. The ground game is the only solution to the problem, and since your feet may slide under you, you seldom can get set for great speed. Now is the time when control, and mixed spin and direction really come into their own. The greatest attack on a slippery court is varied depth—alternate short and deep shots. The most consistent winner is a sudden shot back to the place a player has just left, since to stop and turn on a slippery court is extremely difficult. However, to make this winner effective, you must use the corner-to-corner placement first to get your opponent moving. Mixed spin shots are also very tough to handle on a slippery court, since proper preparation is hard to achieve, and proper preparation is the only way to meet mixed spin successfully.

The Rough, Uneven Court Surface. This will produce bad bounces in such numbers that it makes impossible the usual method of judging the bound. Playing on this type of court, once again you must take the racquet head back and have it ready at the earliest possible moment, but hold the actual shot until the last second, in order to be ready in case of a bad bound. The backswing should be short, and the same sort of intense concentration is required as is the case when playing in the wind.

However, the best solution for beating the problems offered by a really rough court surface is to go to the net at every opportunity. Follow service in consistently, and also, whenever possible, go in on your return of your opponent's service. In other words, play the ball in the air, before it has a chance to bounce, as often as you can. Certainly, it is taking chances to go in to net so much, but you are taking at least equal risks in staying back and having to face the bad bounces that will surely annoy you. Don't let bad conditions upset you and ruin your game. Realize that they are just as bad for your opponent, and if you can combat them intelligently and effectively, you can make them assets in a match.

The Entire Tournament Program. A wise player always takes a look at the draw, in a tournament, and figures out whom he will probably meet in each round, if he wins. This is not conceit, but merely common-sense preparation. However, once you have looked over the possibilities, then play each match at a time without thinking about the future ones, except as they fit into the whole picture. Often a player has his mind so intent upon how he will play some star in the semifinal that he gets licked by some comparative dub in the second round, just because he forgot that he had to beat him first. He could have won if his mind had been on his match, but he was two days ahead of time, thinking of the star. It only takes one defeat to put you out of a tournament, no matter who you are, so keep your mind on the match at hand until it is over and won, and then begin to think about your next opponent.

With that word of warning, I will go on to the real point of this particular section, which, at first glance, may seem a little contradictory. But it isn't. If you don't lose sight of the fact that each individual match must be won before you can play the next one, you can start thinking generally in terms of the entire tournament program.

You should always try to so pace yourself, time your game, and prime your condition, that you play your best tennis when you need it, in the important matches of the biggest tournaments. Don't waste your very best on pushovers in early rounds of small tournaments. You don't need an elephant gun to kill a squirrel. I remember Jack Dempsey once saying that the stamp of the champion was his ability to be right at ten o'clock on the night of September 8th in Madison Square Garden, when the championship fight started. Not at nine o'clock or eleven o'clock, but at ten o'clock. That may be an oversimplification, but it's a deeply searching exposition of the quality that makes a champion in any sport. It's the ability to be right at the moment when the stakes are highest, the pressure greatest, with a title itself at stake. That is what a player must try to learn to do all through a season. By learning it in each tournament, you gradually learn to do it all the time, bringing your game to a peak at the great tournaments, and letting down a bit in between. One reason why I believe that Pancho Gonzales will be a great performer for years to come is that, in 1948 and 1949, although his record was marred by many minor losses, he produced when he had to, and won all the important United States championships, on every type of court surface. That shows true championship quality to a remarkable degree.

You must play every match with enough concentration on it alone to win, even if you think it's going to be easy for you. But you must save your peak of physical condition and your ultimate tennis talents for the times when you are going to need them most.

CHAPTER 16

Maintaining Pressure on
Your Opponent

THE HABIT of establishing and holding pressure on a tennis adversary will pay big dividends. So many players bear down only in fits and starts. An early lead will give many a player a sense of false security, and cause him to let up, when actually he has nothing more than a slight advantage due to his opponent's starting slowly. The match actually has not yet begun. The letup may be fatal, because once a man has relaxed his pressure and let his opponent get started, he often finds it impossible to lift his game again and stop him. The place where most players are likely to throw away matches is about the middle of the second set, in a two-out-of-three-set match. A man has taken the first set, leads at perhaps 3-1 or 4-2, and decides that the match is as good as over. He stops concentrating, plays carelessly for a few moments, and before he realizes it he has lost his service. His opponent holds his service and the game score is tied, but now the man who led a few short minutes ago senses his danger and starts thinking how foolish he was to let up on the pressure. The other man is buoyed up by the reprieve, senses his opponent's uncertainty, and it apt to break through the first man's service again, and run out the set. If he does, the entire complexion of the match is changed. Now the strain is on the man who threw away the lead, and unless he has a remarkably good match temperament he is likely to blow up and throw away the third and deciding set. Until you have won the last point of a match, there is no time when you are completely out of danger, if you let up. I know this only too well from many sad personal experiences. I cannot too strongly stress the absolute necessity of concentrating and keeping the pressure on, no matter how big your lead, or how helpless your opponent may appear. Win first, and then be sympathetic. Don't get sorry for him too soon, or you may wind up being sorry for yourself.

This leads right into one of the most intricate aspects in the study of tennis, but one which is of inestimable value to the person who really appreciates it, and plays with it always in mind.

Playing to the Score.   Every point in a match is naturally important but there are certain points in each game, certain games in each set, and certain sets in a match that are crucial. The player who knows those points and games, and makes special effort to win them, will greatly increase his chances of victory. The crucial points in a game are the third and the fifth. The crucial games in a set are the fourth, particularly the seventh, and the ninth. The crucial sets are the first, in a two-out-of-three match, and the third, in a a three-out-of-five match.

While understanding the psychology of these vital moments in tennis, never lose sight of the fact that every point, game, and set counts, and you must play to win them. Do not think that you can play carelessly at other times, if you play well at the critical stages. What I mean, in stressing them, is that you should exert extra effort at these times.

Consider the third point of a game! Your score is given first. The score stands 30-0, 15-all, or 0-30. In the first case, if you win the next point it gives you 40-0, and you will win that game about nine times out of ten. If, however, the score is 15-all, then the point means the advantageous position to you at 30-15 (or at 15-30, if you are receiving), from which you can press on to game. At 0-30, if you win the third point you still have a life—not too good, but still a chance—whereas if you lose it and are 0-40, then you have only about one chance in ten for the game.

The fifth point means that the score stands at 40-15, 30-all, or 15-40. Here you are playing a point which, in two cases, actually means the game, while in the other case you are both fighting for a very important advantage. Certainly, if you're ahead at 40-15, you cannot afford to be careless, since a lost point will make it 40-30, and one more point won by your opponent evens the game at deuce. Yet many players play that 40-15 situation with an air of having such a commanding lead that they need not worry about it. I see more games booted away by a careless, half-concentrating shot at 40-15 than at any other time, and second to that is at 30-0, where the situation is fairly similar. The necessity for special effort on the 30-all and 15-40 situations is so obvious that I need do no more than point it out.

There are many psychologically important games. For that matter, every game is important, and no player should throw one away by carelessness or inattention. The psychological effect of winning the very first game, particularly if you can break your opponent's service, may determine an entire match. If you possibly can, break your opponent's first service game, and hold your own. Still, the chips are not really down until about the fourth game. Here is the first big psychological moment in game score.

Let's look at the possibilities. The score may be 3-0, 2-1, 1-2, or 0-3. This next game really puts it up to you. If you win it and lead at 4-0 (in the first instance), you hold a double service break and will win the set an overwhelming majority of times. If you lead at 2-1, you are playing to establish or to hold a service break, and to stay in the lead at the halfway point in the set. This is a big advantage that may well make your opponent "press" in an attempt to recover. But if he wins this fourth game you are all even, with the psychological edge to him, particularly if he broke your serve to do it, since he has cut down your lead. If you are on the short end of 1-2 or 0-3, the reverse of all the above is true, and you must win the fourth game to stay in the set.

Strange to say, the psychological advantage of winning the fourth game is greater than that of the fifth or sixth, although both the latter are important, but the really big moment comes in the seventh game.

The set usually hangs on it. The score is 5-1, 4-2, 3-all, 2-4, or 1-5. Since the set ends, if the player leading at 5-1 wins the game, you can forget that situation. With that lead he will almost always win the set anyway. It is the 4-2 situation that is so vital, particularly if it is on your own service. Here you have the chance to push your opponent into an almost hopeless position. If you win this seventh game, he must win three games in a row to get even to a deuce set, a far from pleasant prospect. On the other hand, if he breaks your service, he is within a game of being even, with his own service to follow. Encouraged by his success in breaking your delivery, he will probably reach 4-all easily. Once more, you will have allowed the psychological edge to get away from you and pass to him. Always make your greatest effort to consolidate a 4-2 lead. The 3-all situation explains itself, since you are both fighting for the obvious advantage on the first step after the halfway mark of the set. If you are down 2-4, you must win that game to stay in the set, as shown conversely above.

The ninth game often winds up the set, of course. The score is 5-3, 4-all, or 3-5. Since a victory for either man with five games means the set, I need only say, win it at all costs. The 4-all situation is where you are fighting for the set itself. If you win, the pressure on your opponent is greatly increased, since he will have his back to the wall in the next game, and every point will practically amount to set-point. If you lose that ninth game, then you will be the one who will be fighting for his life. Give all you own in the ninth game, and if you win it, many times your opponent cracks and the tenth is easy.

It goes without saying that every set is of extreme importance. Any time you drop a set you are in danger, but in a two-out-of-three-set match, the first set usually carries the victory with it. I believe that the man who wins the first set wins 80 per cent of the two-out-of-three-set matches played. If you are a set in, your opponent is placed under the tremendous pressure of knowing that he cannot afford to let you have a chance at another. Therefore, he is forced to work at top speed all through the second set, which, even if he wins it, may well take such a toll of his physical and nervous reserves that he will have nothing left in the third set. In a three-out-of-five-set match, the climactic set, in my opinion, is usually the third. The first is naturally of great psychological value, but it is not actually decisive. If you can win both the first two sets, so much the better. Still, the third set is the critical one. If the score is 2 sets to 0, a victory in the third means the match. If you are behind at 0-2, you must win the third or the match is lost. But in many three-out-of-five-set matches, the players divide the first two sets and stand at 1-all. Now the real importance of that third set comes to the fore. If you win it and lead, 2 sets to 1, the discouragement to your opponent is tremendous. By the end of a third set, any player will be feeling the physical strain, more or less. To face the necessity of winning two sets in a row places a great burden on the mental and physical courage of your opponent. It looks like an awfully long road back. You may even be able to afford taking the chance of running him in the fourth set and, even if you lose it, tire him so much that he will be easy in the fifth. It is, of course, better to keep pressure on in the fourth set, and take no chances.

If your opponent leads you 1-2, then it's up to you to muster all the guts you have, go out for a quick victory in the fourth set, and then shoot the works in the fifth, even if you wind up flat on your face at the end.

There is much more to playing to the score than just learning what points, games, and sets are crucial. You must know how to put the pressure on your opponent in the most effective and winning way. Putting pressure on an opponent is not just hitting hard and rushing the net. There are many other ways, just as difficult for him and much safer for you. The method should be determined by the situation. When you have a commanding lead, and an error will cost your opponent a vital point, perhaps even a game or set, give him every opportunity to make it. Keep that ball going back to him at all costs and always, if possible, to a new place so that he must move to reach it. Every time he hits the ball he is aware that, if he makes an error, it's costly, and each return you send back to him makes him more and more nervous and tense. If he should give you a weak mid-court return, which he is very apt to do under pressure of that kind, then attack it deep, not too hard, very safe and sure, and go in behind it!

Pass the buck to him. Now he must take a chance or lose, for if he defends, you have the kill. He will probably go all out for his shot and miss. Whenever you have your opponent where he cannot afford to take a chance, keep the ball going back and vary spin, speed, direction, and depth consistently, but never so much that you are in real danger of missing. Give yourself plenty of margin. Only if you have an exceptional chance should you attempt to win outright. Do not let him off the hook by making errors yourself. Make him earn his way off, if he can, by the sweat of his brow and his own good shots, because, if he should get off, he will have a psychological uplift that will make him very dangerous.

Always use your service aggressively at the crucial moments of a match, if you are behind. If you are ahead, be certain that your service keeps your opponent on the defensive, but you need not give it quite so much as when you are behind. When you are in the hole and fighting for your life, remember that your opponent will not expect you to attack, so do so the first *logical* chance. Do not take *unnecessary* risks, though you must risk enough to surprise and upset your opponent if you are ever to pull up from behind and win.

Many a player plays a set-point or a match-point to him or against him, and doesn't realize that anything crucial is going on, because the score does not say so. I mean by that, the final result of many sets and matches hangs upon points which come up early in the first set. Let's take a hypothetical situation, which illustrates very nicely the crucial-point and crucial-game theory I have discussed in this chapter.

Two players, of almost equal ability, are battling in a match that each is very eager to win. Both men are keyed up and inclined to be jittery. Mr. A. leads, 4-2 and 40-15 on his own service, and feels he has the set in hand. On the next point Mr. A. reaches the net, and Mr. B. hits him an easy drive which, if Mr. A. played carefully, he could put away for a win. Instead, without taking proper care, he attempts a drop-volley, and misses the shot: 40-30 instead of a won game and a 5-2 lead. Annoyed, Mr. A. goes back and serves a double fault. Deuce. Mr. B., cheered up by these two reprieves given him by Mr. A., makes two fine shots and the score is now 3-4, with Mr. B.'s serve coming up. He is back again in the match, and he eventually wins it. Actually, if Mr. A. had played his 4-2, 40-15 volley carefully, he would have won the game, and probably the set and match.

In my opinion, the match-point was that missed volley, but neither man knew it at the time. So keep alert for the psychological value of certain points, played early, and sense the possibility of the equivalent of set-point, or match-point, coming up for you when you least expect it. Many a match can be turned by taking advantage of the unexpected reprieve, or the lucky break in your favor. Always be on your guard against giving your opponent another chance he hasn't earned. Consolidate your gains whenever you pile up an advantage, and be ready to jump in and grab an opening if it's given to you.

CHAPTER 17

Doubles and Mixed Doubles

EVERYTHING that I have said up to now about strokes, tactics, and so forth has had to do with playing singles. The singles game is the acme of tennis skill because it allows the widest range of attack and defense, strokes, tactics, and psychology, but the doubles and mixed doubles games have their own charm and fascination. Many people enjoy doubles more than singles, probably because they have to do less work, have a partner to blame for defeat and someone to listen to their gripes as they play. It fills their social need far better than singles. The mixed doubles game, while a completely unbalanced and, in many ways, uninteresting game, still brings sex and beauty on the court—that is, if you're lucky enough to have Gertrude Moran or someone like her, if there are any, as your partner.

Just why I should write of either doubles or mixed doubles will probably remain a mystery, since during my long career I successfully defended the title of "the world's worst doubles player" over all comers throughout that time. The title was wished on me by Harold H. Hackett, a great doubles player of the past, who added the potent comment that I "parked my intelligence outside the stadium" because I dared to disagree with Mr. Hackett's idea of how doubles should be played in a Davis Cup match against Australia. The fact that R. N. Williams, II, and I won that Davis Cup doubles match, and that I won the United States Doubles Championship five times with three different partners, did nothing to change Mr. Hackett's views or deprive me of my title. Personally, I disagree completely with Mr. Hackett's valuation of my doubles, and, without fear, I am going to attempt to give an idea of the doubles and mixed doubles games.

Doubles and singles are quite different games in the manner in which you use the shots of tennis. Singles is essentially a baseline game, with occasional net attacks. Doubles is a net game, with as little back-court play as possible. Singles is a game of ground strokes; doubles is service, volley, and smash, with the ground stroke an added necessity in returning service. Singles is the game of moderation, average pace, with peaks of great power or subtle finesse. Doubles is a game of extremes. It is all terrific attack, or slow, delicate finesse, with practically no average-pace shots. This is largely because there are smaller openings on a doubles court; two men are covering very little more territory in doubles than one does in singles. So you must take greater chances to get shots past them.

In the old days, doubles found one team at the net with the other on the baseline, attempting to force them back and advance themselves. But they did not do so until they had forced the other team back. Today all four men are in at the net most of the time. The server's partner naturally stands in, and the server naturally follows his service in. That has been standard for years. Today the receiver's partner stands in, and the receiver attempts to follow his service return to the net, thus bringing all four men to close quarters on practically every point. It certainly breeds brilliant, sensational tennis, which thrills the gallery, sets a tremendous pace, eliminates long rallies, and piles up amazing numbers of errors and some incredible placements. But I wonder what would happen to this type of doubles against such great doubles teams of the past as William M. Johnston and C. J. Griffin, the Kinsey brothers, R. N. Williams, II, and Vincent Richards, George Lott and Lester Stoefen, Wilmer Allison and John Van Ryn, Ellsworth Vines and Keith Gledhill, Donald Budge and Gene Mako, to say nothing of such foreign pairs as Henri Cochet and Jacques Brugnon, Jean Borotra and Jacques Brugnon, Gottfried von Cramm and H. Henkel, F. J. Perry and G. P. Hughes, Jack Crawford and Harry Hopman, or Gerald Patterson and Norman E. Brookes.

Somehow I feel that these teams of former days would have too much combined attack and defense for the modern game, and it would show up again that, even in doubles, the attack is overemphasized today.

Doubles always is, or should be, a service battle. Service gives the attack and the net to the team serving, and that advantage should win them the game. One break through service usually settles a set in doubles. Once that is recognized, then obviously the most important shot in doubles becomes the service return. I am absolutely certain that any team that will put every service in play will win any doubles match. The average team today tries to do too much with the service return, and to follow in behind it, with the result that something like 50 per cent of their service returns are missed in the great majority of games. If they are lucky and happen to get a streak of good shots in one game, they may get a break, but most of the time the server wins so easily that it puts no pressure on him at all. The most effective service return in doubles requires little more than control. All you should set out to do is hit the ball cross-court hard enough and sharp enough so that the net man can't "poach" and reach it, but that is all. Let the server make his volley if he can. Do not try for a clean winner, or for such terrific speed that the server can't handle it, because if you do your percentage of errors will be much too high. The first great rule of good doubles is "Make 'em play it," which means, put your service return in and start the point, put the burden back on the server. Once the service is in play, then you should go out to win at the earliest moment.

Second only to the importance of the return of the service is the use of the lob. This shot, which today is almost extinct in singles, is the favorite and, in fact, almost the only defense in doubles. Even off service you will find the lob often played. It should usually be tossed with a general cross-court tendency to the deep middle of the opponents' court in defense. This type lob may have a tendency to make the other team uncertain which of the two players should handle it, whereas the straight shot should always be handled by the man over whose head the toss is made. The lob should always be smashed in the air if it is possible to reach. Do not drop it, and smash it off the bounce, since,

1. It is harder to time.
2. It drives you farther back into your court.
3. It gives you less angle.
4. It gives your opponents the chance to take the net away from you.
5. It leaves your partner alone at the net.

In doubles, the lob-volley, made when all four men are close in at the net, is a very valuable variation of the volley. It should be played sparingly, since it must have a surprise element to win, and unless it wins outright it is fatal, since it is just a setup for a kill.

Never forget that doubles is a team game. Every time you hit the ball, you must take into consideration not only your position but also that of your partner. You cannot afford to play a shot that may save you if by so doing you put your partner in an untenable position. Doubles position is largely one of mutual understanding. There are a few general rules for teamwork that can be learned, but on any individual point they may have to be thrown away, and one of the men must call on that peculiar thing known as "anticipation" to save the situation. Here are a few generalities:

1. A doubles team works as a unit but not quite on a line. The player on the side with the ball in front of him is a few feet closer to the net and directly in front of the ball in play while his partner covers the center of the court from a point about two feet deeper. Should the next shot to them go back to the other side of the court, then the man who was in the middle moves in toward the net and directly in front of the ball, while his partner now drops a few feet back and moves into the center of the court.

2. The man closest to the net, usually in front of the ball, should step in, even poach any time he sees he can reach a ball for a kill, no matter how far he may go into his partner's territory, but if he does poach in front of his partner, he must end the point, win it or lose it. It is inexcusable not to put the ball away, because he will

have opened his side of the court. If he cannot reach the cross-court shot for a kill, then he should let the cross-court go to the man covering center. He is in position.

3. Unless caught off balance, each man should cover his own overheads, even if he is compelled to drop the ball, run back, and play it off the bounce. If he is compelled to do this, his partner should drop back into the center of the court or he will be left in an untenable position if the opponents come in, which they should.

4. If for any reason your partner crosses behind you to play the overhead calling "Mine!" to show he will play it, let him. Hold your position and do not cross, *except* when your partner calls "Cross!" as a signal to you.

This is in conflict with most experts, who advise the automatic cross, but I have logical reasons.

a. If you stay where you are, your partner knows where you are and then can play his shot with that in mind, so that he knows just how far he must go back to cover his court.

b. Only one man will be moving and out of position, leaving only the wide opening cross-court undefended, whereas if you too are moving, neither of you is in position. So the entire court is now vulnerable, particularly through the middle between you.

c. You are in position to poach after the cross-court if you want to take a chance on a kill.

d. If your partner calls "Cross!" go into the center of the court and stay in close to the net. Watch for the shot between you. The return will usually go there.

5. Either man must always feel free to cross in front of his partner or go anywhere in the court out of logical position if by so doing he can make a kill. The only thing is, he *must* go out for that kill if he commits himself.

The one absolute necessity for a good doubles team is the mutual give-and-take attitude of the players. They must have confidence in each other, complete faith that each is doing his best at all times, and each must be willing to overlook any errors of commission or omission

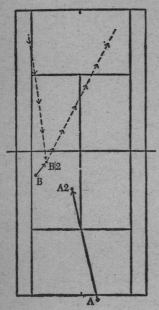

NET POSITION IN DOUBLES

These diagrams show a typical example of how a doubles team works at the net. *Solid line—movement of players; broken line—flight of ball.*

A serves and comes in toward the center of the court to A2.

B, his partner, is at net. B steps in to B2 and cuts off the service return, volleying it off to the opposite side of the opponents' court.

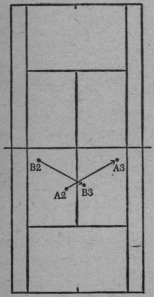

Continuing the situation:

As A sees B hit this volley, he moves over and in toward the net to A3, in front of a probable return by an opponent, while B drops back a few feet and moves into the center of the court, from B2 to B3.

Should A's net volley, from A3, go straight back down the sideline, A and B would hold their respective positions at A3 and B3.

But should A's net volley be cross-courted back to the opponents' other court, then B would move back to his position at B2, and A would move back almost to A2.

of his partner. Nothing can beat a team quicker than friction. Open griping is inexcusable, of course, but that air of resigned martyrdom that is so obvious (and, I regret to say, popular) with some players is just as disastrous. Once in a long while a player will really "throw" his partner, and "dog" a match, but such situations are few and far between. If your partner does that and you know it, I suggest defaulting the match, walking off the court, and never again stepping on a court with that man. I am a great believer in two partners' talking to each other, encouraging each other, and working always with a show of friendship. I think it has a definite effect, not only on your partner, to keep him happy and working, but also in making the other team aware of your co-operation toward victory. Do not always try to get the best player as your partner, if you and he are not compatible. You will not be a good team. Usually two great singles players together do not make a great doubles team. Each is too apt to be an individualist, who wants to run the team, with the result that they never achieve smooth teamwork. They remain two fine singles players, playing singles side by side on a doubles court, but they are not a doubles team. Examples of that were Donald Budge and Bobby Riggs, or Henri Cochet and Jean Borotra. Budge and Mako were a far finer team than Budge and Riggs, yet Mako was never the great player that Riggs was. Cochet with Brugnon, and Borotra with Brugnon, were both better teams than Cochet and Borotra, yet Brugnon was hardly in the same class as the other two. I have always believed that the really great teams were made up of a clever, steady player who made the openings, and a hard-hitting killer, who won the points through those openings. It is always the killer who gets the reputation, but it is the man who makes those openings who is the wheel horse of the team and its real strength. It was Mako who gave Budge his chances. Peck Griffin opened for Billy Johnston, John Van Ryn gave Wilmer Allison his openings, George Lott worked out the setups that Lester Stoefen put away. Among modern players this art is almost lost. Only Frank Parker has the quality that made Mako, Griffin, Van Ryn, Lott, and Brugnon among the greatest doubles players in history. Those men are great doubles partners with any hitter.

Get one thing firmly fixed in your mind about playing doubles. You can't blast your way from the baseline through a doubles team in position at the net. There are two men to cover only thirty-six feet of width on the court. There just isn't room enough, until you have moved one or both of them enough to open their court. What are the various ways to open up the holes? They are few but definite. You must go outside, between, or over your opponents, but you can't hit through them from back court.

To open the court by going on the outside of the team two shots are logical:

1. The straight passing shot down the alley past the player in front of you, which, if played, must be a fast flat drive.
2. A slow cross-court, sharply angled shot, which can be either a slow drive, flat or topspin, or a slow slice.

Both shots must be low and short. The straight shot, either off service or in play, verges on an attempt to win, and is always very aggressively hit. It should not be played as often as the cross-court, since to succeed it needs an element of surprise. The cross-court shot is definitely an attempt to make the opponents volley up so you can win on the next shot, and does not carry the same chance to win outright as does the straight shot.

The most used, and certainly the most popular, shot is the one down the center between the two opponents. There are several reasons for this:

1. It is easier to hit and carries less risk of error.
2. It may cause uncertainty between the other two men as to which should play it, so that perhaps both men will let it go, or both will try for it and clash, either of which tends to break up their teamwork and confidence.
3. It provides less angle for the opponents to hit for, and is apt to give you a chance for a winner on the next shot to a sideline, since both men have been pulled in to the center.

If you decide to open up the court by going over the opposing team, the only shot is the lob. It is difficult to drive a team away from the net by lobbing but it can be done. Lob *high* and *deep* and *often*, but the

132

moment you sense a tendency in your opponents to hang back and wait for the lob, shift at once to the drive and go in yourself. If at any time you succeed in getting a lob over your opponents' heads, so they are compelled to drop it and hit it off the bound, go in to the net at once, one player closing the straight shot and the other closing the center of the court. Give them the cross-court angle to hit at. They will make one and miss ten, trying it.

Once you have made an opening in your opponents' court in doubles, go out for your shot at once. There is not time, or room in the court, to continue maneuvering them around. Remember always that average pace, except on your service return, is not good. It calls for increased speed, or a really slow delicate pace, to win. Every shot that you play should have the definite object of either winning outright or assisting you in gaining the net position where you can win outright. Doubles is a game of much less depth to the ground strokes than singles. The sharp-angled shot, the fast-dropping drive, the short, slow slice, are used far more than the full long sweeping drive or deep-floating chop. The tempo of doubles is much faster than singles, and many more risks should be taken. In general, doubles shots are made with a shorter backswing from a position closer in on the ball; often they are even hit on the rise, particularly on return of service. This is due to the necessity to get to the net if possible. There is little defense in doubles, beyond the use of the high lob.

There is one extremely valuable tactic for doubles. That is to decide which of your opponents is more apt to break, then start from the very beginning of the match to pick on him. Play him continuously, cutting his partner out of action as much as possible. This will result in the man you play tiring, nervously and physically, while his partner is apt to get overanxious and make the mistake of attempting to play shots he would do better to let alone. This may cause friction between the players and break up their teamwork.

If you find a hole in a doubles team, pick on it every chance you get, because nothing will break up the morale of a team so quickly as for one man continually to miss the same shot. The place where most teams break is overhead, and if you start one man missing his smashes, lob him to death. Lob to him at every logical chance. An overhead, more than any other shot, depends on confidence. Once you shatter a player's confidence, you will see his overhead lose all its sting if it does go in, but most of the time it will miss. If you find a player with a really weak service that sits up and asks to be hit, then I suggest picking on his partner at the net. Pound the ball by him, and also right at him. You will find that his volley will quickly break up under the barrage, and a spirit of unrest will invade their team, particularly on the weak service. A doubles team is a little like a dam that holds back water. One little crack in the solidarity of the team, and quickly the breach widens until a flood of errors carries them down to defeat.

Mixed doubles is well named. It is neither fish, flesh, nor fowl. The moment you attempt to pit a man and a woman against each other on equal terms on a tennis court, something goes lopsided somewhere. No woman ever has been or ever will be able to play on equal terms with a top-flight man. She may be just as good a tennis player, hit a ball with as good strokes, and know as much about the game, but from a purely physical angle she can't hit as hard, run as fast, or last as long. Only two women have ever approached playing even with men in mixed doubles. They were Suzanne Lenglen and Alice Marble, who could come to the net and volley and smash with the men, owing to their remarkable speed of foot. Even the incomparable Suzanne and Our Alice, great as they were, could not quite meet the requirements of the greatest men. Such marvelous stars as Helen Wills Roark, Helen Jacobs, Pauline Betz, and the two best women doubles players in the world today, Margaret Osborne du Pont and Louise Brough, are not in the class with the top men in doubles. Therefore, mixed doubles, with a team made up of a man and a woman, must necessarily be a lopsided and a rather unequal game. There is always a great discussion raging as to where the woman should play, and how much she should do. I endeared myself to all my mixed doubles partners by answering the question of where she should play quite truthfully—wherever she would be least in the way. The whole theory of winning at mixed doubles is rather unfair and definitely ungallant.

134

It is that the first time the man gets the ball he should hit at the other woman as hard and in as difficult a position as possible. A nice clean-cut gentlemanly attitude! Still, if women insist they are men's equals, and want to play us on our own ground, there's nothing to do but accept the challenge.

Mixed doubles in Europe and in the United States are played entirely differently, and you can take your choice of which way you think is better. In Europe, the woman hangs back on the baseline, while the man charges in to the net and attempts to volley or smash every shot he can get a racquet on. The woman scurries around like a rabbit behind him, and lobs the ball back sky-high whenever she has to chase one that got past him. Once in a while she drives, just to prove she can. This form of mixed doubles produces long, bitter struggles, usually ending with all contestants on the verge of exhaustion.

Here, in the United States, the girl is planted firmly at the net, told to stay there, not move too much, and to stick a racquet against any shot that comes near her. The man now is covering all the back court, coming in whenever possible, and also definitely playing all the over-heads over the girl's head that are deeper than the service line. This form of mixed doubles results in the physical exhaustion of the man, but it greatly aids the general aesthetic quality of the game, for the girl can usually remain cool, calm, collected, and, at times, beautiful. Once in a while you find a girl who really gets into the game and plays her one third of the match, which is all any sane man would allow her to play. Such girls are Louise Brough, Margaret Osborne du Pont, Doris Hart, Gertrude Moran, Patricia Canning Todd, Virginia W. Kovacs, Nancy Chaffee, Beverly Baker, Helen Pastall Perez, and a few others. This lifts the game into the spectacle class, and galleries love it. Nothing so cheers up a gallery as for one of these gals to get a nice setup and smash it past, or directly at the opposing man. The fact that a ten-year-old would have won the point means nothing. The gallery yells itself hoarse.

There are few general tactical rules for mixed doubles, since the game is too uncertain in class, but there are a few:

1. Hit at the girl whenever possible.

2. A sudden shift down the man's sideline, particularly if made by the girl, will often pay.

3. One player up and one back, which is fatal in men's doubles, is a safe and, at times, sound formation in mixed. Take your pick of who's up and who is back.

4. The lob over the girl's head is one of the best shots in mixed doubles, provided you play it far enough to her side so that she has to cover it or make the man run a long way to save her.

5. The middle shot in mixed is not so good, since the man is usually covering center court.

6. Speed to the girl, finesse to the man, will pay in the mixed game. Remember that a girl's fastest shot is a man's average pace, so if you use real speed against her, it will prove a tremendous pressure under which she is apt to break. The man is tuned to speed, so fool him by finesse.

There is one thing about mixed doubles that you must remember in these days. The modern girl in athletics is going to handle men's shots better than you'd expect. The girls of today practice so much with men that they are tuned to greater speed than they themselves can hit. Such girls as Gertrude Moran, Louise Brough, Nancy Chaffee, Beverly Baker, etc., play infinitely better tennis in practice against men than they ever do in matches against each other. Because of this, all these girls are apt to play extremely well in mixed doubles, where they are hitting many of their shots off men's speed.

With this glimpse into the doubles and mixed doubles games, I have fairly well covered the actual playing of tennis from A to Z. If I have managed to get over the point that there is a much wider field of technique and brainwork than the present school of tennis uses, I have carried my message to you. There is still much to learn. Some of you may want to teach the game, professionally or on an amateur basis. There are definite ways of teaching tennis that will get results. Some of those I have tried to explain. We have a great future for tennis in the United States, if we will develop our youth soundly. We are a champion nation today, but that is due more to the war and its effect on other nations than it is to our real strength. The other countries will come back strong. Let us be stronger. We have a group of young players today who, while good, could be still better, while our players of tomorrow need a tremendous amount of hard work and a new goal to strive toward. Let us set out to make the Champion of Tomorrow the greatest champion in tennis history.

PART FOUR · THE SUMMING UP
CHAPTER 18

The Coaching Job

ONE HEARS a great deal about the proper attitude of the public toward learning, but it is seldom that anyone says very much about what the teacher's approach to his job should be. It seems to me that the success or failure of many pupils rests at least as much in the hands of the teacher as in themselves. Teaching tennis is not an easy job if you want to get results, and anybody who thinks it is has my full permission to try it out for a while. It is hard, serious work, physically, mentally, and nervously, if a person is conscientious about it and gives of his best all the time. Unfortunately, there are no requirements for becoming a tennis professional. All it seems to take is a tennis racquet, tennis clothes, and a desire to make a living. There are hundreds of such self-called professionals in America. The United States Professional Lawn Tennis Association is fully cognizant of the situation, and is doing all in its power to stamp out the incompetent professional. There are many capable and hard-working professionals who will give valuable instruction to their pupils. Most of these teachers are members of the U.S.P.L.T.A. Membership in that body is one guarantee of the qualifications of the coach that will at least insure a sound, if not necessarily brilliant, teacher. There are a limited number of recognized teachers in the coaching profession who stand out like beacons. A young player cannot go wrong if he goes to any one of them. The greatest tennis coach in the United States, in my opinion, is Eleanor Tennant. "Teach," as she is known to one and all, is the person who is responsible for the championship career of Alice Marble. She aided Mary Arnold Prentiss, has done much for Helen Pastall Perez, and advised Gertrude Moran and, to some extent, Bobby Riggs. Miss Tennant's ability to diagnose immediately what is holding a player back in his game and her uncanny knowledge of the quick and correct cure make her unique in my experience. I feel that Miss Tennant is a better coach for women than for men, but anyone will benefit from her coaching. She is now in Los Angeles.

Lester Stoefen, the famous Davis Cup doubles player, is coach at the La Jolla Beach and Tennis Club in La Jolla, California. "Stoef" is second only to Eleanor Tennant as an analyst and diagnostician. He is the best service coach in the game, and is my choice for men who desire to have their game sharpened up for tournament play. I cannot begin to go through the entire list of the proven coaches, but certainly such men as Dick Skeen in Los Angeles, who has produced Louise Brough; Ed Faulkner in Philadelphia, George Agutter in New York, George O'Connell in Chicago, Howard O. Kinsey in San Francisco, and others, can be engaged with confidence in the results. Do not go to a coach of whom you know nothing, and personally I do not advise going to some of those much-publicized alleged professionals, who have never played tennis at any time in their lives. I believe a good teacher must be able to play at least well enough to give any of his pupils practice. He does not have to be a champion, or even a first-rate player, but he does have to be able to play well enough to demonstrate the strokes to his pupils, and then be able to keep the ball going so they can practice.

What must a really good coach be able to do?

1. He must have a complete knowledge of the mechanics of any shot he coaches.
2. He must be able to explain it lucidly.
3. He must be able to demonstrate its execution.
4. He must have the patience to go over the same thing any number of times, until it is learned.
5. He must have enthusiasm for his job, because only by that can he keep his pupil's interest. If he is bored or uninterested in his work, it gets over at once to the pupil, who immediately lets down.

6. He must have sufficient personal interest in his pupils to treat each one as an individual. I think many coaches make the mistake of attempting to make every person play the same way. This is wrong. Each pupil is an individual problem to be handled slightly differently. The foundations of technique must be taught the same to all, but the expression of those fundamentals should and will vary slightly with each person.

7. He must be able to make the science of the game reach and appeal to the mind of the pupil, so that the pupil will know the why, as well as the how, of the technique. If he fails, all he gets out of the pupil is a bad imitation of his own game, with nothing behind it.

8. He must always give full value for his pay, not only in time but in effort. Only by this can he hope to keep his pupil's enthusiasm and continued patronage. He cannot afford to be late for appointments or cancel them without good cause. On the other hand, he must hold his pupil up to the same standard, otherwise he cannot command the pupil's respect.

9. He must be ready and willing to answer questions on the game, because nothing is healthier for a pupil than the curiosity that prompts them. If the coach is too busy or too lazy to answer, the pupil's interest will again waver, and once more a valuable asset is lost.

10. He must get results as fast as is consistent with solidity, and when the time comes for a pupil to go on his own for a while, tell him so frankly rather than keep him dangling on. The greatest advertisement in the world for a coach is a player who goes out and says, "See what I learned in ten lessons," if he has really improved. It's much better than the pupil who never gets anywhere in fifty hours, even if the latter paid more.

The most important quality a coach can have is the ability to keep the interest of his pupils in learning the game. I have had the pleasure of working with many famous people in various artistic activities, and I found that my greatest asset was the fact that I could usually translate the thing about tennis I was trying to get over to them, into terms of their own work. At once they had an added interest in the game. They began to think about it and analyze it themselves, and there was immediately established a sort of partnership between us. We no longer had a pupil-teacher relationship, but rather that of a couple of people attempting to work out a problem together. I had one sort of special knowledge that I contributed, but they also were working with me. Once you appeal to a person's intellect, he feels an equality of effort that will make both his job and yours much easier.

I believe that the only way to get satisfactory results is to be completely frank with a new pupil. I always ask a person at the first lesson how much tennis he has played, and just what he wants done. If he is a complete beginner, I tell him frankly it will take him at least twenty lessons before he has enough of a game to start to play. I also tell him that it will be about six months before he reaches a point where he gets much real fun out of playing, but that is variable and depends largely on his efforts during those first lessons. I figure that during those first twenty lessons I can teach him to hit a service and forehand into court with regularity, and give him a reasonable start on a backhand. Anyone who promises quicker results is either an optimist, a miracle worker, or a liar. I urge the pupil to pick a time when he can concentrate on learning tennis, and not spread his time out. I want to get at least three, and preferably five, days in succession, to lay the foundation of forehand and service, which I teach in that order. This is because the physical groove of the stroke can be set only by daily use in its early stages. After the groove is fairly well set, then twice or three times a week will do, but I am convinced that one lesson a week is money thrown away. I am certain that the more intensive the work—daily is best—for the twenty hours, the better. It will pay the biggest dividends. Personally, I do not want one of my pupils to attempt to play or practice alone, without my supervision during the first ten hours, because the groove of the strokes is not set. In his keenness to win or to play well, he sacrifices form to result, and destroys most of the constructive work we've done together. For the first five days, I will not allow him to run or move over one or two steps for a ball, since to do so upsets footwork and body control. Once I have managed to bring a pupil to the point where he can begin to move to forehand and backhand shots in succession, and can put at least 50 per cent of service in play, I advise him to play other people all he can. I am apt to suggest that he stop lessons for a month, and

140

then come back to me again to be checked and corrected on what has developed during that month of play. I feel that all beginners need to gain a sense of self-sufficiency, and not rely too greatly on a coach. At the same time, they must go back for repairs, or they will probably throw away most of the game they originally learned, since it has only partly jelled and must be solidified again.

I believe that a coach should be completely frank and truthful with a pupil about his progress or lack of it. I see many coaches who have nothing but praise for pupils who actually need a good bawling out. They are not giving value, in my opinion. On the other hand, there is the coach who never has anything to offer but criticism. This is even worse, for it has the definite effect of destroying the morale and confidence of the pupil. This is particularly true with children, who need encouragement and praise if it's due, and they know it's sincere. I do not hesitate to praise, but also I will not stand for lack of effort. The only thing that no coach should allow is half-hearted effort and attention. Much as I appreciate the value of the money that would have come to me, I have several times sent pupils away and refused to coach them again until they had reached the conclusion that they would really work. A few never did come back, but in most cases they returned soon and with an attitude that made progress really rapid.

Coaching beginners will always present a tremendous psychological problem to the coach. Almost all beginners are very self-conscious and the first great hurdle lies there. The coach must find some way in which to draw the pupil out of himself so far that self becomes quite secondary to hitting the ball. I usually spend a few minutes talking about tennis, then try to find out what other games the pupil plays. If possible, I translate what I am attempting to teach in tennis into terms of the other sport. I take up the grip and the swing of the racquet, with the correct footwork stressed. I get the pupil to go through the shot "in shadow" without the ball, try to get a bit of a laugh out of it somewhere, and then set a ball in front of him and tell him to hit me. For some reason I think I will not explore too deeply, this seems to strike a responsive chord, and the pupil forgets himself enough to take a real swipe at the ball. If he hits it, which he usually does if he has listened to instructions, the satisfaction more than makes up for any self-consciousness, and we're off to learn tennis.

The grind is during the first few days when you must continually correct the fundamentals, particularly that of keeping the eye on the ball. You must catch these errors of eye or foot or slow backswing *every* time, not just now and then. To do it without irritating the pupil, or depressing or confusing him, often presents a problem. I have found that kidding gets the best results. I am apt to inquire, "Who's your friend up in the tree?" when he looks up, or "I appreciate the compliment but don't look at me," when his eye wanders. Once you have brought the beginner to where the form of the shot approaches something that looks pretty sound, then your problem is to get control by stabilizing the swing. To do this you must make the pupil play the shot over and over and over. This is, naturally, a more or less boring proceeding, particularly to the average youngster, yet it is absolutely necessary. I always get around some of the monotony by making a game out of it. I "play" them one hundred shots at a time. They "win" all their good ones, I "win" all they miss. I never return a ball, just set it once in front of them from across the net: first one hundred forehands, then one hundred backhands, and I end with one hundred services. When they get to the point where they can hit better than 70 per cent of them in, I get them to try it out at different speeds and in different directions. I call

60 per cent to 70 per cent	Fair
70 per cent to 80 per cent	Good
80 per cent to 90 per cent	Excellent
Over 90 per cent	Super

You would be surprised how interested a pupil becomes in bettering his record, and what remarkable results you can get once that interest is caught.

My next step is to go back to the baseline and see how many times we can keep a ball going from the back court without missing. After he gets reasonable control anywhere in the whole court, I then make it forehands only, or backhands only. The next step is forehand cross-courts only, then forehand straight shots. That is followed by the same routine on the backhand. As you can see, this type of practice is all to establish control, and is getting into a fair class of tennis.

10 in a row is fair
20 in a row is good
30 in a row is excellent
50 is super

It is far more difficult to use this kind of practice for the net game, but the net game is for advanced players so the problem of holding attention is not so pressing an issue.

When you come to the matter of coaching more advanced players, your problem is a very different one. Here it is largely a matter of having it understood who is the teacher. I have had many fair tennis players come to me and say they wanted lessons, that this or that in their game needed work, and God only knows it did, but as soon as I set out to do the necessary work on it, they began to teach me. The only way I have successfully coped with that particularly irritating specimen of tennis nut was to play a match, pick on the weakness, and break it up so utterly that even the owner of it could not doubt it. Then, perhaps, he would listen to reason. If that doesn't work, give it up as a bad job; nothing can be done.

When a player is tuning up for a tournament, a coach should find out what particular shot or shots he wants to practice, or against what type game, and then play him, giving him always the type practice he wants without worrying about score or even thinking of the result. You are there, not to prove you can win, but for the sole purpose of tuning up the other player's game, and that is what he is paying you to do. A good coach should never allow personal pride to stand in the way of doing the job he is paid for. If he wants to prove his ability, he should do it some time when he is not taking money for a job.

A club professional should always be working to know as many as possible of the club members and their relative abilities. He should try to be in a position to arrange matches at short notice for members who have no game and want one. To do this successfully, he should be able to rate all his players in their proper relative classes. Nothing is more distressing to some players than to find themselves in a game with players much too good or much too bad for them. It requires tact and judgment to be able to arrange matches, but a pro who can do this well is a great asset to a club and very popular with the membership. The pro should be willing occasionally to "fill in" for fun himself if no fourth is available for doubles and there are three players waiting, but he should not make a practice of it, unless he is paid his regular price per lesson. The professional coach has an important place in the tennis game. He can give much for the money he is paid, but I am sure that in addition to that, he should always be willing to give free, without thought of return, all that he can of his knowledge, to any boy or girl of exceptional ability. I know that I am proud of what little I have been able to do to help the tennis game by working for nothing at clinics, and sometimes with individuals.

I am hoping that some of the results of that coaching will be seen in the near future in the games of my current protégés, and that the tennis philosophy in this book contributes to the return of the balanced, intelligent game. If either of these ambitions of mine are realized, and I do help restore the game I love, I can feel it is the climax to my tennis, and can lay down my racquet with a sense of complete contentment and fulfillment.